HOPI
KATCINAS

HOPI
KATCINAS

by
Jesse Walter Fewkes

DOVER PUBLICATIONS, INC.
New York

Published in Canada by General Publishing Company, Ltd., 30 Lesmill Road, Don Mills, Toronto, Ontario.

Published in the United Kingdom by Constable and Company, Ltd., 10 Orange Street, London WC2H 7EG.

This Dover edition, first published in 1985, is an unabridged republication of the work first published by the Government Printing Office, Washington, D.C., in 1903 as a paper contained in the *Twenty-First Annual Report of the Bureau of American Ethnology to the Secretary of the Smithsonian Institution, 1899–1900*. The plates appeared in color in the original edition. The index in the present volume is adapted from that of the original edition, which covered all papers in the *Report*.

International Standard Book Number: 0-486-24842-9

Manufactured in the United States of America
Dover Publications, Inc., 31 East 2nd Street, Mineola, N.Y. 11501

CONTENTS

Page

CONTENTS 9

ILLUSTRATIONS

11

INTRODUCTION

The Hopi Indians represent their gods in several ways, one of which is by personation—by wearing masks or garments bearing symbols that are regarded as characteristic of those beings. The symbols depicted on these masks and garments vary considerably, but are readily recognized and identified by the Indians.

At each festival in which these supernatural beings are personated the symbols are repainted, and continued practice has led to a high development of this kind of artistic work, many of the Indians having become expert in painting the symbols characteristic of the gods.

Believing that a series of pictures made by the cleverest artists among the Hopis would be a valuable means of studying the symbolism of the tribe, the author hired one of them to make him a series of drawings of all the personations of supernatural beings which appear in Hopi festivals. This method was suggested by an examination of Mexican codices, especially the celebrated manuscript of Padre Sahagun, now in Madrid, the illustrations in which are said to have been made by Indians, and Chavero's Lienzo de Tlascala, lately (1892) published by the Mexican government.

The author found several Hopi men competent to paint a collection of pictures of the kind desired, and finally chose for that work Kutcahonauû,[a] or White-bear, a man about 30 years old, who was believed to be the ablest of all who were considered. This Hopi had picked up a slight knowledge of English at the Keams Canyon school, and while his method of drawing may have been somewhat influenced by instruction there, this modifying influence is believed to be very slight, as the figures themselves show.

---

[a] For the pronunciation of proper names, see the alphabet at the end of this paper.

His uncle, Homovi, who has never been to school, and is unac-
quainted with the English language, drew some of the best pictures,
the technique of which is so like his nephew's that it is safe to con-
clude that the drawings of the latter are aboriginal in character. A
few of the pictures were drawn by Winuta, whose work, like that of
Homovi, is unmodified by white influence. A boy who had attended
a Government school in Lawrence, Kansas, also made a few paintings, but as they show the influence of instruction in this school they
are not valuable for the purpose had in mind in publishing this collection, and they have not been reproduced here.

While, then, their character has possibly been somewhat influenced
by foreign art, the pictures here reproduced and described may be
regarded as pure Hopi, and as works little affected by the white
teachers with whom of late these people have come into more intimate
contact than ever before.

To facilitate the painting the author provided the artists with paper,
pencils, brushes, and pigments; he left the execution of the work
wholly to the Indians, no suggestion being made save the name of
the god whose representation was desired. They carried the materials
to the mesa, and in a few days returned with a half-dozen paintings,
which were found to be so good that they were encouraged to continue
the work. In some instances, the artists painted pictures of gods
which the author had never seen personated.

When the paintings were delivered, the author wrote under them
the names of the beings represented, with such information as could
be gathered concerning the special symbolism upon them. Later
other Hopis were asked to identify the pictures, which they readily
did, the names they gave being nearly always the same as those given
by the artists. This independent identification was repeated many
times with different persons, and the replies verified one another almost
without exception. The talks about the paintings elicited new facts
regarding the symbolism and the nature of the beings represented
which could not have been acquired in other ways. Several men made
critical suggestions which were of great value regarding the fidelity
of the work and embodied information which is incorporated in the
exposition of the collection. At one time the reputation of these
pictures was so noised about in the pueblos that visitors came from
neighboring villages to see them. At first the collection was freely
offered to all comers for inspection, on account of the possibility that
new information might be thus gathered, until some person circulated
a report that it was sorcery to make these pictures, and this gossip
sorely troubled the painters and seriously hampered them in their
work, but the author was able to persuade the artists and the more
intelligent visitors that no harm would come to them on account of
the collection.

The pictures were made primarily to illustrate symbols and symbolic paraphernalia used in the personation of the gods, but incidentally they show the ability of the Hopis in painting, a form of artistic expression which is very ancient among them. The painting of figures on ancient pottery from Tusayan, illustrated in a collection from Sikyatki, leaves no question of the ability of the ancient Hopi women in this form of expression.[a] As specimens of pictorial art the pictures here presented compare very well with some of the Mexican and Mayan codices. They represent men personating the gods, as they appear in religious festivals, and duplicate the symbols on certain images, called dolls, which represent the same beings. A consideration of some of the more characteristic dolls in semblance of gods is given elesewhere.[b]

When a Hopi draws a picture or cuts an image of a god, either a doll or an idol, he gives the greatest care to the representation of the head. The symbols on the head are characteristic, and its size is generally out of proportion to that of the other parts. When these same gods are personated by men the symbols are ordinarily painted on masks or helmets; consequently the heads of the figures may be said to represent masks or helmets of personators.

The personations which are here figured generally appear in winter festivals or ceremonies, a more detailed account of which will be given elsewhere, but it has seemed well to preface this description of the pictures with brief summaries of great festivals in which the figures represented are specially prominent, and to make such reference to others as may be necessary. The great festivals, called Pamürti,[c] Powamû, and Palülükoñti or Añkwañti, are celebrated in January, February, and March.

The personations are called katcinas; the nature of these merits a brief consideration.

Primitive man regards everything as possessed of magic power allied to what we call life, capable of action for good or evil. This vital power, he believes, is directed by will; it was probably first identified with motion. To the savage whatever moves has a beneficent or malevolent power, sometimes called medicine, the action of which is always mysterious. Various symbols have been adopted by primitive man to represent this power, and many terms are used to define it. Among these symbols words for *breath* in various languages are perhaps the most widely spread among different races. The power of motion directed by will to do harm or good thus comes in English to be known as spirit or soul. The doctrine of medicine power or of spirits is commonly called animism.

---

[a] See Archeological Expedition to Arizona in 1895, in the Seventeenth Annual Report of the Bureau of American Ethnology, part 2, 1899.

[b] Internationales Archiv für Ethnographie, Band VII, 1894.

[c] For the pronunciation of proper names, see the alphabet at the end of this paper.

Early man rarely generalized. Every object, organic and inorganic, had a spirit, but these spirits, like the objects themselves, were thought of as concrete. The spirit of the tree had little in common with the spirit of the sun. To distinguish these differences symbolic personifications were called in, and the medicine power of objects was embodied in objective comprehensible form; thus the medicine power of the sun presented itself as an eagle, that of the earth as a spider.

It would appear, also, that in case of the magic or medicine power of man, there was a universal belief that it existed and was potent after death. The breath-body or spirit of man was believed to have a continued existence after the death of the body, retaining powers of good and bad action, a belief which led to worship. The katcinas are spirits of the ancients of the Hopis, and personations of them by men bear the symbols which are supposed to have characterized these ancients.

While the term katcina was originally limited to the spirits, or personified medicine power, of ancients, personifications of a similar power in other objects have likewise come to be called katcinas. Thus the magic power or medicine of the sun may be called katcina, or that of the earth may be known by the same general name, this use of the term being common among the Hopis. The term may also be applied to personations of these spirits or medicine potencies by men or their representation by pictures or graven objects, or by other means. As applied to a dance in which the personations appear, the term is secondary and derivative.

The word "medicine" is here used in its ancient meaning, not as in modern English. It is misleading to apply such terms as "spirit," "soul," and "medicine," with the modified meanings which they now have, to beliefs of primitive man. When these words originated they were applicable to such beliefs, but in the evolution of culture their meanings have changed, and they are now symbols of beliefs that are very different from those which they originally represented.

In the Hopi ritual there are dramatic celebrations of the arrival and departure of the katcinas. Certain clans have special festivals in which they dramatize the advent of their clan-ancients; thus the Katcina clan represents it in a festival called Powamû, the Asa clan in Pamürti, the Patki clan in Soyaluña. Kindred clans unite with the more prominent in the dramatization of the advent of their clan-ancients. There is only one dramatization of the departure of clan-ancients, a festival which is called the Niman (departure), and which occurs in July. Personations of the same clan-ancients do not appear every year at a stated time; in some years they are more numerous than in others, as quadrennially, when certain initiation ceremonies are performed. Particular personations are prescribed for great festivals like Pamürti, Powamû, and Palülükoñti, and these appear yearly, but there are others whose appearance depends on the inclination of the owner of the masks or on other causes, on which account the personnel of the actors in the festivals changes year by year without, however, there being any fundamental modifications.

The author has repeatedly been informed by the Hopis that the number of katcinas is very great, much greater than the number figured, especially if all those mentioned in traditions are included. When we reflect upon the probable way these supernaturals have been added to the Hopi Olympus, we may gain some idea of their possible number, for each clan as it joined the Hopi population brought its own gods, and, as the clans came from distant pueblos, where environmental conditions differed, each had a mythologic system in some respects characteristic. Many Hopi clans have in course of time become extinct, and with their disappearance their old masks have passed into the keeping of kindred clans, to whom they are now known as "ancient," being never used. The distinctive names of such have been lost, but in some cases the mask still retains its symbols. Then there is a constant increase in the numbers of katcinas; not only are the Hopis acquainted with many katcinas that are no longer personated, but they are also continually introducing new ones. Thus the katcinas called Chicken, Cow, and many others which might be mentioned, have made their appearance in the last decade. It is not difficult to see how this may have been brought about. A man goes on a visit to Zuñi or some Rio Grande pueblo and witnesses a personation of a katcina which, on returning to his own home, he introduces into the Hopi ritual. This process of introduction has been going on for many years, so that we have katcinas called Navaho, Kawaika (Keresan), Pima, Apache, and others of foreign derivation. Thus not only have clans introduced new katcinas from time to time, but individuals have done the same, and in many instances this introduction has taken place so lately that the name of the man who brought them is known, as he is still living in the pueblo.

Of the masked personations among the Hopis some, as Tuñwup, Ahül, and Natacka, always appear in certain great ceremonies at stated times of the year. Others are sporadic, having no direct relation to any particular ceremony, and may be represented in any of the winter or summer months. They give variety to the annual dances, but are not regarded as essential to them, and merely to afford such variety many are revived after long disuse. Each year many katcinas may be added to any ceremony from the great amount of reserve material with which the Hopis are familiar. Some have become extinct, and knowledge of them remains only in the memory of old men, or now and then one may be recalled to mind by an ancient mask hanging in a darkened room. Thus, it is seen that within certain limits a change is continually going on in the character of the personations in masked dances.   It is more especially to the ancient or almost forgotten varieties that we should look for aid in making a classification of katcinas.

The pictures have been arranged primarily on a basis of the sequence of appearance in the annual calendar.   Possibly a more comprehensive classification of the pictures might be made with reference to the clans which introduced them, and tables are given with that thought in mind, but there is little possibility that a classification of this kind can be made complete, since the clan origin of many katcinas will always remain unknown.

The classification of katcinas by names leads to important results, but the nomenclature, for many reasons, is often deceptive.   The same god may have several attributal or clan names which have survived from the different languages spoken originally by component clans of the tribe.   Certain peculiarities of song or step of the personator, or a marked or striking symbol on his paraphernalia, may have given a name having no relation to the spirit personated.   Keeping this fact in mind, and remembering the permanency of symbols and the changeability of nomenclature, we are able to discover the identity of personations bearing widely different names.

An important aspect of the study of these pictures is the light their names often throw on their derivation.   We find some of them called by Zuñian, others by Keresan, Tanoan, Piman, and Yuman names, according to their derivation.   Others have names which are distinctly Hopi.   This composite nomenclature of their gods is but a reflection of the Hopi language, which is a mosaic of many different linguistic stocks.   No race illustrates better than the Hopi the perpetual changes going on in languages which Payne so ably discusses in the second volume of his History of America.   The successive clans which united with the original settlers at Walpi introduced many words of their peculiar idioms, and it is doubtful whether the present Walpians speak the same tongue that the Snake (Tcüa) clans spoke when they lived at Tokonabi, their ancient home in northern Arizona.

HOPI FERIAL CALENDAR

PECULIAR FEATURES

The author will first sketch the ferial calendar[a] of Walpi and give a brief account of the nature of the rites occurring each month, having especially in mind the personages here figured; but only so much of this calendar will be given as will help to explain the pictures and render the paraphernalia intelligible.

---

[a] For ferial calendar of the Hopis, see Internationales Archiv für Ethnographie, Band VIII, 1895, pp. 215, 236; American Anthropologist, vol. XI, 1898; Fifteenth Annual Report of the Bureau of Ethnology, 1897, p. 260 et seq.

The ceremonial year of the Hopis begins in November with a New-fire ceremony which assumes two forms, elaborate and abbreviated. The elaborate form, given every fourth year, is very complicated, owing to the initiation of novices into the fraternities. Following this precedent, the rites of the winter solstice (Soyaluña), Powamû, and Palülükoñti are celebrated in extenso in those years. The elaboration or abbreviation of the New-fire ceremony, which opens the calendar, thus profoundly affects all festivals of the remainder of the year.

There are also several other variations in the calendar, due to the celebration of either the Snake or Flute festival, which alternate with each other. Thus in odd years there is in January an assemblage of the Snake fraternity, while in even years the Flute priests have a meeting in the same month. There are likewise certain minor modifications in other ceremonies in those years in which the Flute and Snake ceremonies, respectively, are celebrated.

It must be borne in mind that the Hopis are ignorant of the Roman names of months, January, February, and the like, but these names are introduced in the following pages for convenience in reducing their calendar to our own. Their months often take the names of the ceremonies which occur in them.

The four seasons, spring, summer, autumn, and winter, have no equivalents among the Hopi so far as is known. The Hopi year has two divisions, which may be designated that of the named and that of the nameless moons; the former is the cold period, the latter is the warm—roughly speaking, they are winter and summer. These divisions may be called the greater and lesser periods, as the former begins in August and ends in March. In the first occur the greater, in the other the lesser mysteries (see below, Classification of Festivals), although this practice is sometimes reversed.

CLASSIFICATION OF FESTIVALS

As has been noted, the ceremonies in the Hopi calendar vary in complexity as a result of the initiation of novices into the priesthoods, which occurs about every four years.

In addition to this quadrennial variation there is a lesser and greater celebration of the same festival each year, which are ordinarily six months apart, the lesser being generally in winter. The adjective "elaborate" will be applied to those quadrennial festivals which are celebrated in extenso, "abbreviated" being applied to the smaller celebrations in intervening years; the two yearly presentations will be known as the greater and lesser mysteries.

ELABORATE FESTIVALS

Some of the elaborate festivals involve nine days' active work, others five.   In years when the New-fire ceremony is brief, other nine-day ceremonies are abbreviated to five, and five-day ceremonies are shortened to one.   A list of the festivals of the latter class is given below, under Abbreviated Festivals.

Among elaborate festivals with a nine-day duration may be mentioned the following:

Naacnaiya.	Leleñti (Leñpaki).
Soyaluña.	Lalakoñti.
Powamû.	Mamzrauti (Maraupaki)
Niman.	Owakülti.
Tcüatikibi (Tcüapaki *a*).	

With the exception of Powamû and Niman the above festivals have two additional ceremonial days called the smoke talk and the public announcement days.   The ceremonial days of these elaborate festivals are called:

First day: Tcotcoyuñya.	Fourteenth day: Yuñya.
Second day: Tiyuna.	Fifteenth day: Cuskahimû.
Tenth day: Yuñya.	Sixteenth day: Komoktotokya.
Eleventh day: Custala.	Seventeenth day: Totokya.
Twelfth day: Luctala.	Eighteenth day: Tihüni.
Thirteenth day: Naluctala.	

The days between the announcement (second day) and Yuñya (tenth day) are generally seven in number, but may be less.   The nine active days begin on the first Yuñya and end on Tihüni, the public dance day, which is followed by three or four days of purification.   Practically each of these ceremonies takes twenty days from the smoke talk (Tcotcoyuñya) to the final day of purification.

ABBREVIATED FESTIVALS

Among five-day ceremonies which are believed to be contracted forms of the first group, may be mentioned:

Wüwütcimti.	Palülükoñti, or Añkwañti.
Pamürti.	

The one-day ceremonies, which may be extended over five days in special years, are as follow:

Winter Flute prayer-stick-making.	Winter Marau prayer-stick-making.
Winter Snake prayer-stick-making.	Summer Sun prayer-stick-making.
Winter Lakone prayer-stick-making.	Winter Sun prayer-stick-making.
	Momtcita.

---

a Literally, snake (tcüa) going down (pakit), referring to entering the kiva.

Tabular View of Festivals in a Hopi Year

The following ceremonies, celebrated annually at the East mesa of Tusayan, are mentioned with the months in which they occur, beginning with the New-fire or November festival.

November, Kelemüryawû (Novices' Moon)

⎰Wüwütcimti (New-fire ceremony).
⎱Naacnaiya (with initiation of novices).

November is generally considered the opening month of the Hopi year, and on the character of the New-fire ceremony, whether elaborate (Naacnaiya) or abbreviated (Wüwütcimti), depends that of the following festivals, for if the former is celebrated the winter ceremonies which follow are always more complicated.

December, Kyamüryawû

1. Soyaluña (All-assembly, Winter-solstice).

Synchronous meeting of all clans in their respective kivas with altars and prayers to Muyiñwû, the germ god. An elaborate sun drama occurs in certain kivas during the festival.

2. Momtcita (war dance of the Kalektaka or warrior priesthood of the Pakab clans).

Stone images of the Hano warrior gods, corresponding to the Hopi Püükoñ hoya, Paluña hoya, and their grandmother Kokyan wüqti (Spider woman), are displayed at the winter solstice ceremony (called Tañtai by the Tewas). At Hano the rites of these gods are combined with those of the germ gods, but at Walpi they are distinct, following Soyaluña.

In this festival there is an altar and prayer-stick-making. The Hano warrior altars are erected in the same rooms and at the same time as those of the Winter-solstice ceremony.

January, Pamüryawû

1. Pamürti.

A dance celebrated at Sichumovi by the Asa and Honani clans, dramatizing the return of the sun, followed by their clan-ancients or katcinas, called by Zuñi names.

2. Leñya or Tcüa paholawû (Flute or Snake prayer-stick-making).

Winter or lesser Flute or Snake prayer-stick-making. The Flute or Snake fraternity of the under world is supposed to meet at this time, and there is a sympathetic gathering of Flute priests in even years and Snake priests in odd years. In the odd years certain rites occur in the kivas during the Soyaluña ceremony to harmonize with the preeminence of the Snake chief in those years.

3. Mucaiasti (Buffalo dance).

4. Tawa paholawû (Sun prayer-stick-making.)

Winter or lesser assemblage of the Sun priests.

February, Powamüryawû

1. Powamû (Bean-planting).

A ceremonial purification festival celebrating the return of the clan-ancients of the Katcina clan, in which several other clan-ancients likewise appear.

2. Lakone paholawû (Lakone prayer-stick-making).

Winter or lesser sympathetic meeting of the Lakone priesthood, who make offerings and deposit them in distant shrines.

March, Ücümüryawû

1. Palülükoñti, or Añkwañti.

Theatrical performance or mystery play, illustrating the growth of corn; its purpose is the production of rain.

2. Marau paholawû (Marau prayer-stick-making).

Spring meeting of the Marau fraternity, who make offerings and deposit them in distant shrines.

3. Sumaikoli.

Spring meeting of the Sumaikoli and Yaya fraternities. A festival of short duration in which new fire is kindled by frictional methods.

May, Kyamüryawû

Abbreviated Katcina dances.

Masked personations of different clan-ancients or katcinas, in public dances of a single day's duration, sometimes accompanied with secret rites.

July, Pamüryauû

Niman Katcina (Departure of the Katcinas).

Elaborate celebration of the departure of the katcinas.

August, Powamüryauû

1. Snake dance (Tcüapaki).

In odd years at Walpi, alternating with the Flute festival in even years.

1. Flute dance (Leñpaki).

2. Tawa paholawû (Sun prayer-stick-making).

Prayer-stick-making by the Sun priests.

3. Sumaikoli.

Meeting of the Sumaikoli fraternity.

September

Lalakoñti.

Basket dance of the Patki (Rain-cloud) clans. Meeting of the Lakone fraternity, in which an elaborate altar is erected and a public basket dance is celebrated.

October

1. Owakülti.

Basket dance of the Buli and Pakab clans. Meeting of the Owakültû society, when an elaborate altar is erected and a basket dance is celebrated.

2. Mamzrauti.

Hand-tablet dance. Meeting of the Marau society, when an elaborate altar is erected and a hand-tablet dance is celebrated.

PRIEST FRATERNITIES IN HOPI CEREMONIAL FESTIVALS [a]

Each of the above-mentioned ceremonial festivals is performed by a society of priests and is simple or complex according to the relative strength and social influence of its priesthood. The following lists give the names of these societies and the festivals in which they are specially prominent:

Fraternity	Festival
Aaltû .... Wüwütcimtû .... Tataukyamû.......... Kwakwantû	Wüwütcimti Naacnaiya
Katcina	Pamürti Powamû Abbreviated Katcina dances Niman
Tcüa .... Tcüb	Winter Snake ceremony Snake dance
Leñya................	Winter Flute ceremony Flute dance
Lalakoñtû	Winter Lakone prayer-stick-making Lalakoñti
Owakültû	(?) Owakülti
Mamzrautû	Winter Marau prayer-stick-making Mamzrauti
Tawa................	Winter Sun prayer-stick-making Summer Sun prayer-stick-making
Kalektaka...........	Momtcita
Yaya................ Sumaikoli	Summer Sumaikoli Spring Sumaikoli

[a] For Hopi religious fraternities see Journal of American Ethnology and Archæology, vol. II, 1892.

There are a few other priest fraternities which take part in the celebration of Hopi ceremonies, the most important of which are the Tcukuwimpkya, among which may be mentioned the Paiakyamû (mudheads), Tatcükti (clowns), and Tcutckutû (gluttons). They are intimately associated with the masked katcina observances, in which they generally take part.

DESCRIPTION OF HOPI FESTIVALS

Wüwütcimti, New-fire Ceremony

The festival of the new fire is performed by four religious fraternities or societies called the Aaltû or Alosaka, the Kwakwantû, Tataukyamû, and Wüwütcimtû.

The dominating element in this great yearly festival, which opens the Hopi year, is the worship of the germ god, Alosaka or Muyiñwû. Fire is a living being, a mystery, or spirit, and the creation of fire is symbolic of the creation of life. The making of the new fire may be considered as a kind of sympathetic magic or symbolic prayer for the rejuvenescence of nature, and the various so-called phallic proceedings which accompany it have the same significance. This festival is not regarded as a fire-worship ceremonial, but an aspect of the worship of the mystery or medicine which fire shares with every other living or moving thing, embracing both organic and inorganic objects.

Soyaluña

The winter solstice ceremony, called Soyaluña, All-assembly, is an occasion of many rites in all kivas on the East mesa, the altars in which are described elsewhere. Its main feature is a prayer to Muyiñwû, the germ god, and in one of the kivas certain clans from the south dramatize the advent of the sun god in the form of a bird.

The public advent of this sun or sky god takes place on the following morning, when the bird personation is replaced by a masked man, called Ahülani. This sun god is also called Soyal katcina, from the fact that he appears at Soyaluña. He is accompanied by two maids, called Soyal manas, wearing masks resembling those of Añya katcina manas, who distribute seed corn to the women of the pueblo.

It will later appear that there is the same dramatization of the arrival of the gods in this festival as in Powamû and Pamürti. There is a representation of the return of a sky or sun god, who appears first in the kiva and then on the following morning at sunrise in public, distributing gifts to the people and receiving their prayers.[a]

---

[a] For a description of the elaborate rites at the advent of the sun god in the kiva, see American Anthropologist, 1899 and 1900. The exercises in the Hano kivas, where there are two altars with serpent effigies (see American Anthropologist, new series, vol. I, 1899), are mainly for rain and crops.

On one of the days of this festival men personating many kinds of birds dance together in the Nacab kiva; this dance is repeated in the Powamû festival, when all the bird masks are repainted and the bodies of the participants are decorated with feathers, the wings and tail being attached feathers. The following birds are personated:

Kwahu, Eagle.	Türpockwa.
Keca, Hawk.	Totca, Hummingbird.
Kowako, Chicken.	Pawik, Duck.
Patszro, Snipe.	Monwû, Owl.
Hotsko, Owl.	Kwayo, Hawk.

MOMTCITA

This special ceremony of the Kalektaka, or warrior society, introduced by the Pakab or Reed (arrow) clans, whose chief is Pautiwa, is observed directly after Soyaluña. The society has a special room for its meeting, which is under the old Pakab house and is entered. from the roof. Ordinarily this room, called the Püükoñki or house of the god of war, is closed. The four walls are decorated with pictures of animals, as follows: On the north side there is a picture of Toko, the Mountain Lion; on the west wall is Honauû, the Bear; on the south is Tokotci, the Wildcat, above which is a five-pointed star; and on the east is Kwewû, the Wolf, above which is a picture of the sun. From their positions on the walls these animals may be judged to be the distinctive beasts of these cardinal points. In one corner of this room there is a recess, ordinarily closed by a flat slab of rock luted in place, in which the images of the war gods are kept. At the time of the ceremony these fetishes and a number of old celts, ancient weapons, bows, arrows, and tiponis of the Kalektaka society are arranged in the form of an altar.

Prayer-sticks of peculiar construction are made by the Kalektaka, and there is a dance at daybreak on the day after their manufacture, in which the participants carry guns, bows, arrows, and other war implements.

The rude stone images representing the Hano war gods are arranged in the kivas during the celebration of the Soyaluña, in the manner described in an account of the rites of the winter solstice at the pueblo. They represent the two war gods, the Spider woman, their grandmother, and Wicoko, a giant bird. The warrior celebration at Hano is combined with the winter solstice rites, whereas in Walpi it is distinct, or rather the Reed or Pakab clans have a special warrior celebration.

The three principal images or idols are Püükoñ hoya, Paluña hoya, and Kokyan wüqti, the symbolism of which is shown in the pictures.

There are other images of Püükoñ hoya in Walpi which are brought into the kivas at Soyaluña; as one belonging to the Katcina clan, used in the Moñ kiva, and one of the Kokop clan, used in the Nacab kiva. These are supposed to have been the property of the warriors of these two clans, but there are no special rites connected with them. At Hano the rites of the warriors occur at the winter solstice, when elaborate altars are erected.

PAMÜRTI

The Zuñi Indians are said[a] to claim Sichumovi as one of their towns, and the Hopis sometimes refer to it as the Zuñi pueblo, for the reason that the clans which settled it, mainly the Asa, and possibly also the Honani, came from Zuñi; but of that the author is not quite sure. It is commonly said that the Asa belong to the Tanoan stock and that they migrated from the Rio Grande via Zuñi, where they left representatives called the Aiwahokwi.

The belief of the Zuñis and Hopis that Sichumovi is closely connected with the Zuñi clans is supported by the existence in that pueblo of a ceremony—Pamürti—in which the majority of the personators are called by Zuñi names, and are dressed to represent Zuñi katcinas. In this festival there are neither secret ceremonials nor altars, save those presently to be mentioned, and no tiponis nor society badges, although ancient masks are publicly displayed in certain houses.

The Pamürti at Sichumovi in the year 1900 eclipsed all ceremonies in January at the East mesa, but simultaneously with it dances were performed in the other pueblos. Pamürti celebrates the katcinas' return (ikini) to the pueblo, the personations at Sichumovi mainly representing the ancients of the Honani and Asa clans.[b] In the same manner Powamû is supposed to represent the return of the ancients of the Katcina clan.

The Pamürti opened with a personation of Pautiwa, who in this festival at Sichumovi is the sun god of the Asa and Honani clans. On the opening day of the celebration he went to every kiva on the East mesa announcing that in eight days the ancients would return and the Pamürti would be celebrated. He threw meal at the homes of the chief clans of Sichumovi—the Honani, Asa, and Patki clans—as he passed through the pueblo, a symbolic act analogous to that of Ahül, who in Powamû makes markings of meal on the doorways of all the houses of chiefs.

Eight days after the sun god, Pautiwa, had made the circuit of the kivas as above mentioned, personators of the following beings marched from the Sun spring up the trail into Sichumovi:

Pautiwa,	Sun god.
Tcolawitze,	Fire god.
Cakwa Cipikne,	Green Cipikne.

---

[a] Mrs Stevenson informed the author that the Zuñi claim one of the towns on the East mesa, and later he learned that the town referred to is Sichumovi.

[b] See Journal of American Ethnology and Archæology, vol. II, 1892.

Sikya Cipikne,   Yellow Cipikne.
Hakto.
Huik.
Hututu.
Caiastacana,   Long horn.

The men who personated these beings gathered about 4 p. m. at a house of the Badger clan on the Zuñi trail, far out on the plain— and there dressed, putting on their masks and other paraphernalia. They then marched in procession to the Sun spring (Tawapa), where they were joined by Walpi men, who came from the Moñ and Nacab kivas. Those from the Moñ kiva represented Helilülü, Kwahu (Eagle), Kwayo (Hawk), Macikwayo (Drab Hawk), Pawik (Duck), and many mudheads or clowns; those from the Nacab kiva contributed several personations of Tcakwainas. The procession, enlarged by these additions, re-formed and continued on up the mesa, under lead of the sun god personation, Pautiwa, past the Rabbit-ear shrine (Sowinakabû) to the Sun shrine, on the east edge of the mesa, mid-way between Walpi and Sichumovi. On their arrival there they re-formed in platoons and continued on to the latter pueblo.

The procession entered the pueblo about sunset, presenting a most barbaric appearance in the rays of light from the western sky. The numerous masked men walked in platoons, wearing painted helmets, those representing birds prancing backward and forward, raising their arms, to which feathers were attached to imitate wings; there were also platoons of men with painted bodies, wearing horned knobbed helmets closely fitting their heads, singing songs and shaking rattles. Prominent among all was a naked boy, painted from head to foot with spots of different colors. He was called Tcolawitze and carried in his hand a cedar-bark torch, one end glowing with fire. The most startling figure was perhaps that representing the Humis katcina, or rather the Zuñi supernatural of this name. He was accompanied by a relative, called their uncle (taamû), and two others known as the Avatc hoya or Little Spotted Ones. These danced together with a full chorus on the following day in the plaza of the pueblo.

There was also on this day a dance in which more than twenty men, personating the Duck or Pawik katcinas, appeared in line in the same plaza. The procession entered Sichumovi back of Anawita's house, continuing along the row of houses on the east side, toward Hano. Turning westward at the north end of the row it passed into the plaza of the pueblo, where it divided into four groups, each of which sought one of the houses of the four chief clans, soon to be mentioned, where receptions had been prepared.

At intervals along the route of their march through the pueblo six temporary shrines had been erected, consisting of a few upright stones inclosing a prayer-stick. Connecting these shrines a line of sacred meal was drawn on the ground, along which line the procession passed. As the personators arrived at each of the six shrines they performed a dance near it, and the leader scattered prayer-meal on the prayer-stick. Each of the four divisions of the procession went to one or another of the following houses: Asa clan house (Homovi's), Honani clan house (Nuvasi's), Patki clan house (Tcoshoniwû's), and Kükütc clan house (Sikyahonauû's).

These houses had been specially fitted up for the reception of the incoming guests, and as they arrived they danced, passing in rotation to the other houses, and so continuing throughout the night.

As each group entered a house, it tied a stick with attached feathered strings in the rafters, after which the katcinas doffed their masks, the men smoked and prayed, and a feast was served. At the close of the feast the women and children began to assemble, filling all available space in the rooms, each family seeking the clan with which it had social affiliation.

There were no elaborate altars in these rooms, but at one end, on the floor, there were masks and other sacred objects belonging to the clan. In the floor of the room at that point there was a round hole called the sipapû, corresponding with a similar opening in the floors of the kivas. The walls of the Asa room were decorated with whole new buckskins nailed in a row about them. The mural decoration of the Kükütc clan was a ceremonial kilt painted on the four walls. All floors were carefully swept and the wealth of the clan was prominently displayed, the clan fetishes being placed on the floor near the symbolic opening mentioned above.

The most important of the latter in the home of the Honani clan were four masks of Wüwüyomo and four masks of the Zuñi Calakos. These were arranged in two rows, one behind the other. Near this double row of masks the men representing Cipikne, Hakto, and Hututu set their masks. The author supposes that the four masks called Wüwüyomo (see plate v), which are apparently very old, as their name indicates, represent sun masks, and as such are symbolically and morphologically the same as that of Ahül, the sun god of the Katcina clan. They are exceptional in having the curved snout (which is homologous to an eagle's beak) turned upward, for in masks of other sun gods which have this organ it is turned downward.

The four Zuñi Calako masks, which the author believes are also symbolic sun masks, are of modern introduction into Tusayan, and do not differ in symbolism from those of the Calakos at Zuñi, from which they were modeled.[a]

No ancient masks were displayed in the house of the Asa clan, but

[a] This is not the place to point out the resemblance between the symbolism of the Calako masks and those of the sun, but the author is firmly convinced that the Calako giants represent giant sun birds. Not only the symbolism but also the acts of these beings support this theory. The Calako festival is practically a sun drama.

near a small opening in the floor representing the sacred region of the room, the men personating Cipikne, Hakto, Caiastacana, and Tcolawitze deposited their masks.

In the house of the Patki clan there was what might be called a rude altar. At one end of the room, on a space a few feet square, the floor had been carefully sanded, and on the sand five rings were drawn side by side with meal. Within each of these rings there was a conventional symbol of a rain cloud. Bird worship predominates in the cults of this clan, and in these rings of meal the masks of the bird gods, Kwahu (Eagle), Kwayo (Hawk), and Macikwayo (Drab Hawk), were placed. It may be remembered that the personators who wore these masks were Walpi men, and that the Patki is a Walpi clan, as distinguished from the Honani and Asa, which have Zuñi affiliations.

The house of the Kükütc clan, also distinctly Hopi, had, however, a row of twenty Tcakwaina masks hanging on the walls. These were not worn by personators in the procession from Tawapa to Sichumovi, but were prominent in the dances throughout the night.

There were dances in Walpi and Hano kivas on the same night, at the same hour, participated in by unmasked personages—Mucaias taka (Buffalo youth), Tacab (Navaho), Woe,[a] Malo, and others. A dance representing all kinds of birds was performed on the same night in the Walpi Nacab kiva.

WINTER FLUTE PAHOLAWÛ [b]

This is an abbreviated meeting of the Flute priests, occurring in even years and lasting one day, during which a simple altar is made, tiponis are put in position, and prayer-sticks are manufactured. There is no public dance and there are usually no masked personages. The Hopi artist has given no drawing of the Flute priest, but in the collection there is a Leñya or Flute katcina, which sometimes appears.

In the winter Flute ceremony there is no altar, but the tiponis or sacred badges of the Flute chief, Türnoa, the Bear chief, Kotka, and the speaker chief, Hoñyi, are placed in line in a ridge of sand back of the symbolic opening in the floor of the kiva called the sipapû.

In 1900 the Flute chief made the following prayer-sticks:

1. A double prayer-stick or paho, flat on one side, an offering to Cotokinuñwû.

2. Eight ordinary green flute pahos.

Hoñyi made the following:

1. A double paho, flat on one side, with corn-husk packages of meal.

2. Ordinary green flute pahos.

The other men present made each two double green pahos as long as the middle finger.

---

[a] The chevron on the face of this being recalls the eagle and hawk symbolism.

[b] The Snake chiefs meet in odd, the Flute in even, years. There are some variations in all the ceremonies of the calendar connected with the celebration of Flute or Snake dance.

Hani, the Piba-Tabo chief, acted the part of pipe lighter, and, after all the priests had taken their positions around the three badges of the chiefs and the basket-tray containing the prayer-sticks mentioned above, lit two pipes, one of which he passed to Türnoa and the other to Hoñyi.

Eight songs were then sung, which Hani accompanied on a flute. During the first song Kwatcakwa arose, put some meal on a feather which he held horizontally, and made several passes over the sacred objects.

In the second song several rattles made of corn shells were used to beat time, and Kwatcakwa sprinkled the objects with sacred meal. During the third song Kotka asperged these objects with medicine liquid. During the sixth and eighth songs Momi, of the Tcüa clan, arose, and stood before the three sacred badges of the chiefs, twirling the whizzer or bull-roarer, after which he repeated the same act on the roof of the kiva.

At the close of the songs all prayed in sequence, and the rites ended with a formal smoke. The prayer-sticks were given to Sikyabotima, of the Kükütc clan, who ran with them as a courier to the different shrines of the gods for which they had been made.

WAHIKWINEMA, CHILDREN'S DANCE

Two days after the winter Flute ceremony just described, 15 little boys and as many girls, each about 10 years old, performed a simple dance in the Walpi plaza. They were dressed and painted by their elders to represent katcinas, and men· sang for them as they danced like their parents, beating time on a drum. At the close of this exhibition a small boy, one of their number, threw piñon nuts to the spectators from a bag he carried, which gives the dance the name it bears (we go throwing).

MUCAIASTI, BUFFALO DANCE

On the night of January 15, 1900, a Buffalo dance was performed in the Moñ kiva by two men wearing Buffalo masks. Tacab and Woe katcinas were represented in the Wikwaliobi kiva, Malo katcina was represented in the Nacab kiva, and the bird personations, Kwahu, Monwû, and Añwuci, appeared in the Tcivato kiva, accompanied by many mudheads. This was apparently unconnected with the Sichumovi Pamürti or with the rites with which the Flute priests made prayer-sticks, which took place in Walpi on the same day.

In the Mucaiasti or Buffalo dance no altar is erected, but the men who take the part of the Mucaias taka deposit offerings in the Buffalo shrine at its close.

The participants in the Mucaiasti of 1900 were (1) the Buffalo youths, (2) the Buffalo maids, (3) the chorus.

The pictures give a good idea of the paraphernalia of the first two groups, which dance together. The chorus accompanies them with a drum, singing a loud and effective song. During the dance it is customary to discharge firearms and to imitate in a way a hunt of the bison, and this part of the ceremony was formerly carried out in a much more realistic way than at present.

The men of the chorus are gaudily painted, bearing sticks or poles to which ribbons, calico, and feathers are attached.

The Buffalo dance is a foreign addition to the Hopi calendar. It is said to be a Tewan ceremonial dance, and some of the Walpi women say they introduced it into Zuñi. The Hano people claim that their Mucaiasti is the best on the East mesa; in former years it was celebrated with much more éclat than at present. There is a tradition that a Buffalo maid was brought to Tusayan from the Eastern pueblos by the Sun, whose emblem she bears on her back in the dance.

Winter Tawa Paholawû

This meeting of the Sun priests or Tawawimpkiya is a complemental ceremony, at or near the winter solstice, of the summer meeting, which occurs in July.[a] No altars are employed, but a number of prayer-sticks are made and later are deposited in special shrines.

The Winter Sun prayer-stick-making takes place in the same room as the Summer, in a house near the Moñ kiva, under the entrance to the ancestral residence of the Patki clan. The only fetish employed is a rude stone frog, over which is stretched a string extended along a line of meal on the floor, symbolic of the pathway of blessings. The men who participate in this rite are all members of the Patki clan.

Powamû

The Powamû festival, ordinarily called the Bean-planting, is one of the most elaborate of all katcina exhibitions, and at Walpi is controlled by Naka, chief of the Katcina clan. One object of this festival is a purification or renovation of the earth for future planting, but the main purpose is a celebration of the return of the katcinas. The festival differs considerably in the six Hopi pueblos and is apparently most complicated at Oraibi.

PLANTING OF BEANS

In the early days of Powamû, beans are planted in all the kivas of the three villages, Walpi, Sichumovi, and Hano, and forced to grow in superheated rooms until the morning of the final day, when they are pulled, tied in small bundles, and distributed, with dolls, bows and arrows, turtle shells, rattles, etc., to the children, by masked persons from each kiva.

---

[a] See Journal of American Ethnology and Archæology, vol. II, 1892.

On every night from the opening to the close of the festival there were dances, unmasked or masked, in all the kivas of the East mesa.

There are personations in nine different kivas at the same time, and although the author has obtained the names and pictures of the katcinas personated, it was quite impossible for him to witness all these dances.

The unmasked dances of katcinas in the kivas are called by the same name as when masks are worn. Some of them are in the nature of rehearsals. When the dance takes place in the public plaza, all the paraphernalia are ordinarily worn, but the dances without masks in the kivas are supposed to be equally efficacious.

On account of the large number of masked men who appear in Powamû, it is one of the most important festivals in which to study katcinas. The whole ceremony is of from sixteen to twenty days' duration, and will later be described in extenso, but for a proper understanding of the functions of the masked personators a summary is introduced of the events of each day in the celebration in 1900.

On the night of February 1 there occurred in all kivas a series of dances of strange character. They followed one after another in rapid succession, and while they took place in all the kivas, the author witnessed them in only one.

First Act

The first dance was performed by men from the Nacab kiva. The men represented all the birds which the Hopis personate in their dances, and the personations were very good. They wore bird masks, their bodies were painted, and small feathers were stuck on their naked legs, arms, and bodies with pitch. They imitated to perfection the step, cry, and motions of Kwahu (Eagle), Palakwayo (Red Hawk), Totca (Humming-bird), Monwû (Owl), Koyona taka (Cock), Koyona mana (Hen), Yaupa (Mocking-bird) Patszro (Quail), Keca (Hawk), Hotsko (Owl?). Three bees (Momo) were also personated, and the men personating them went about the kiva imitating bees stinging by shooting miniature arrows at the spectators.

Second Act

The Tewa kiva contributed a number of mudheads called Koyimsi (a Zuñi name), who danced and sang, performing certain obscene acts which need not be described.

Third Act

A large delegation of Sio (Zuñi) katcinas performed the third dance, which occurred shortly after that of the mudheads. They came from one of the Sichumovi kivas, and their dance was practically the same as that which has been elsewhere described. [a]

Fourth Act

This act consisted of a dance by men representing Tcakwaina ✓ katcinas.

Fifth Act

One of the Sichumovi kivas contributed to this series a dance by a number of masked men representing Tacab (Navaho) katcinas, who were accompanied by two mudheads or clowns.

Sixth Act

This dance was the most exciting of all the exhibitions in this continuous performance. The dramatis personæ were Tumas, Huhuan, and ten personations of Tuñwup, the flogger, all of whom came from the Moñ kiva of Walpi.

The most exciting event in this dance was a flogging act by the last mentioned. During the dance a ring was drawn with meal on the floor, and one of their number stepped within it, dancing all the while, and two of his comrades struck him as hard as they could with yucca boughs on naked back, arms, legs, and abdomen. Shortly after this many spectators, men and women, stepped forward and received similar floggings on bared legs and arms.

ADVENT OF THE SUN GOD, AHÜL

The Powamû sun god arrives in the kiva, where he is said to rise [b] on the night of February 1. Certain rites attend that event, but his advent in public occurs on the following morning (February 2) at sunrise. The man who is to personate the sun god dresses and masks himself at the shrine, Wala, on the trail to Hano, and just as the sun reddens the east he starts up the trail, guided by the Katcina chief. His dress and the symbolism of his mask can be known by consulting the figure which the artist has drawn of him, but a brief reference to his acts may find a place in the general account of Powamû.

The advent of the sun personator is described elsewhere as follows: [c]

Just as the sun rose the two [Ahül and the chief] visited a kiva in Hano. Stooping down in front of it, Ahül drew a vertical mark with meal on the inside of the front of the hatchway, on the side of the entrance opposite the ladder. He turned to the sun and made six silent inclinations, after which, standing erect, he bent his head backward and began a low rumbling growl, and as he bent his head forward raised his voice to a high falsetto. The sound he emitted was one

---

[a] Journal of American Ethnology and Archæology, vol. II, 1892.

[b] The use of the same word for his appearance and for sunrise is significant. Ahül may be translated The Returning One.

[c] Fifteenth Annual Report of the Bureau of Ethnology, Washington, 1897, p. 277.

long expiration, and continued as long as he had breath. This act he repeated four times, and, turning toward the hatchway, made four silent inclinations, emitting the same four characteristic expiratory calls. The first two of these calls began with a low growl, the other two were in the same high falsetto from beginning to end.

The kiva chief and two or three other principal members, each carrying a handful of meal, then advanced, bearing short nakwakwoci hotumni [stringed feathers tied to a twig], which they placed in his left hand while they uttered low, reverent prayers. They received in return a few stems of the corn and bean plants which Ahül carried.

Ahül and Intiwa[a] next proceeded to the house of Tetapobi, who is the only representative of the Bear clan in Hano. Here at the right side of the door Ahül pressed his hand full of meal against the wall at about the height of his chest and moved his hand upward. He then, as at the kiva, turned around and faced the sun, holding his staff vertically at arm's length with one end on the ground, and made six silent inclinations and four calls. Turning then to the doorway, he made four inclinations and four calls. He then went to the house of Nampio's mother, where the same ceremony was performed, and so on to the houses of each man or woman of the pueblo who owns a tiponi or other principal wimi (fetish). He repeated the same ceremony in houses in Sichumovi and Walpi.

During this circuit Ahül visited the following kivas and clan houses of the three pueblos of the East mesa:

HOUSES VISITED IN HANO

HOUSE	OWNER
1. Tewa kiva	
2. Kolon clan house	Nampio
3. Ke clan house	Pobi
4. Sa clan house	Anote
5. Kisombi kiva	
6. Okuwañ clan house	
7. Täñ clan house	Kalacai

HOUSES VISITED IN SICHUMOVI

HOUSE	OWNER
1. Añwuci kiva	
2. Tcoshoniwû's kiva	
3. Honani clan house	Kokaamû
4. Honani clan house	Kele wüqti
5. Ala clan house	Tüba

HOUSES VISITED IN WALPI

HOUSE	OWNER	TIPONI
1. Kokop clan house	Kutcnaiya	
2. Patki clan house		
3. Kokop clan house	Saha	Marau tiponi
4. Leñya clan house	Sakbensi	Leñ tiponi
5. Moñ kiva		
6. Patki clan house	Vensi	Lakone tiponi
7. Wikwaliobi kiva		
8. Asa clan house	Wuko mana	{Wüwütcim tiponi {Tataukyamû tiponi
9. Kokop clan house	Nakwawainima.	Owakül tiponi

---

[a] Naka became Katcina chief at Intiwa's death.

10. Tcüa clan house	Saliko	Tcüb tiponi Tcüa tiponi Marau tiponi Tcak tiponi
11. Nacab kiva		
12. Patki clan house	Kotsyumsi	Lakone tiponi
13. Honau clan house	Kotka	Aal tiponi
14. Ala clan house	Pontima	
15. Pakab clan house	Nuñsi	Kalektaka tiponi
16. Katcina clan house	Komaletsi	Katcina tiponi
17. Al kiva		
18. Tcivato kiva		
19. Asa clan house	Tuwasmi	Aal tiponi
20. Patki clan house	Naciainima	Lakone tiponi
21. Pakab clan house	Poyaniumka	Sumaikoli tiponi
22. Patki clan house	Nempka	Lakone tiponi Soyal tiponi

After the personator of the sun had visited all these houses and kivas he sought a shrine dedicated to the sun, where he made his offerings and, retiring to a sequestered place, disrobed and returned to the kiva in the pueblo, carrying his mask hidden in a blanket. This personation did not again appear in Powamû.

PRELIMINARY VISIT OF THE MONSTERS

On February 10, in Powamû, a group of monsters (Soyokos) from each pueblo visited every house on the mesa. The object of these visits was to tell the people that in several days they would return for meat and bread. These monsters are called Natackas, and the group from each pueblo consists of Hahai wüqti (their mother), Natacka mana (maid) and Natacka naamû (their father). The members of each group from the different towns are clothed in essentially the same costume, and have the same symbols on their masks.

The acts of Natacka naamû, Hahai wüqti, and Natacka mana on February 10 were essentially the same, each group first visiting all the houses of its own pueblo and then those of families of the other pueblos on the East mesa the heads of which were men of its town who had married and had children.

When it arrived at a house, the group, preceded by Hahai wüqti, halted before the door, and its leader called out in falsetto voice, asking for the inmates. The mother of the monsters carried a collection of snares (small animal traps made of a stick and yucca fiber) and when a man or boy appeared she gave him one, telling him to hunt game, and in eight days she and her company would return for meat. She gave to the women and girls an ear of corn, telling them to grind it, and saying that in eight days the visitors would return for meal and bread. The Natacka father (naamû) said nothing, but hooted and hopped back and forth, assuming threatening postures.

This visit was an announcement to the households that in course of time the monsters would return for gifts, so the males were directed to hunt for meat and the women to prepare paper-bread and meal to give them.

FLOGGING THE CHILDREN

The most important act on February 14 was the child flogging at Walpi and Hano. This is done by two Tuñwup katcinas, assisted by their mother, Tumas, in the presence of people of the town, and is briefly described under the heading Tuñwup.

RETURN OF OTHER KATCINAS

On the same day appear also Hahai wüqti and a number of other katcinas. Many masked men, singly or in pairs, wander about the pueblos, especially by night, during the preceding days. The theory of Powamû is that all the katcinas return, and one comes upon them unexpectedly in all the pueblos. Of many noticed besides those already mentioned, there were several called Wukokoti (big masks; plate xxiii), Ahote (plate xxxvii), and Owanozrozro (plate xxviii). They wander from place to place, accosting pedestrians or calling out at the kiva entrances to the inmates below.

ADVENT OF MASAUÛ

One of the most interesting ceremonials witnessed at Walpi in Powamû was performed on the evening of February 15. It was called the advent of Masauû, and is preliminary to one not seen by the writer, but described by some of the Hopis, which was later performed at or near planting time at Mastcomo, a mound on the trail from Walpi to the Middle mesa. As this rite is not of annual occurrence, and as it may not be witnessed again, it may be described in detail.

On entering the Tcivato kiva about 8 p. m., the author found several chiefs seated in a ring by the fireplace, engaged in a ceremonial smoke. Among these men were Anawita, Sakwistiwa, Winuta, Kanu, Momi, Pautiwa, Haya, Hoñyi, and Türnoa. All smoked for a long time, frequently exchanging terms of relationship.

There were in the room at the same time about twenty other men who were decorating their bodies with white pigment, drawing lines with this material along their legs and arms. They placed daubs of white on their cheeks and tied small yucca fibers in their hair. No masks were seen, but it was gathered from the conversation that some of these men were to personate katcinas, and some were to represent maids. They were called the Maswik katcinas (the Masauû-bringing katcinas) and later accompanied the Masauûs as they went from kiva to kiva.

When these men had finished their bodily decorations, they formed a line near the walls of the room and sang a spirited song in cadence with their dance. As they sang Momi left the room, but soon returned with a mask of Masauû, which he laid by the fireplace within the ring of priests. It looked like a giant skull, but closer examination showed it to be a great hollow gourd, with a large broken orifice and small holes for eyes and mouth. It was not decorated, and was destitute of feather adornment. In places around the broken part the edge appeared serrated. Through the broken opening the head of the man who wore the mask was thrust. At the same time that Momi brought the mask he brought also two old, almost black blankets, two ancient planting sticks, and two basket plaques in which were fragments of piki (paper-bread) and other objects.

Immediately after these objects had been laid on the floor, each of the chiefs puffed great whiffs of tobacco smoke on the mask, after which they prayed very fervently in sequence, beginning with Pautiwa. Songs then began, and as they sang Sakwistiwa took the mask in his hand and squirted over it from his mouth an unknown liquid which imparted a black color to the object. He then sprinkled on the face of the mask a quantity of micaceous iron (yayala) and laid it back on the floor.

Each of the painted men then in turn approached the mask and laid a stringed feather, called a nakwakwoci, in one of the basket trays. They then formed in line and danced to songs, shaking cow bells and rattles, making a great noise. Meanwhile one of the chiefs, in a voice almost inaudible, talked to the mask. So low was his tone that it would have been impossible for one to have understood this address, even if he were well versed in the Hopi language.

When the Maswiks had finished their songs, they filed out of the room and the two men who were to personate Masauû began their preparations. They tied agave (mobi) fiber about their legs and arms, slung the black blanket under one arm and tied it over the other shoulder; each took a planting stick and a basket tray. One of these men then slipped the gourd over his head, and thus costumed they left the room.

Meanwhile the Maswiks, seating themselves on the top of the kiva, were awaiting the preparation of the two Masauûs, and when the latter were ready they filed into the Moñ kiva, where many male spectators had gathered to see the performance presently to be described.

These Masauû rites are performed in each kiva in rotation, beginning with the Moñ kiva. In each of these rooms a considerable number of male spectators had gathered to witness the rites, and the events which occurred in the different kivas were substantially identical. Having seated himself among the spectators in one of the kivas, the author witnessed the ceremony from beginning to end.

As the line of Maswiks came in, a pinch of sacred meal was thrown upon each by the kiva chief. A song then began, accompanied by the bells which the katcinas carried, and soon the personator of

Masauû came down a ladder as if a stairway, and, making his way back of the line of dancers, came forward between two of them and squatted before the fireplace. The second personator followed, unmasked, but with two black streaks painted on his cheeks. He took his seat by the side of Masauû, assuming the posture of a man planting, holding one end of the planting stick to the floor as if it were soil. Thus these two personators remained until the songs ceased, not speaking. When the Maswiks filed out, each said "Good night" but the last one, who carried a bundle slung over his shoulders, halted, with one foot on the lowest rung of the ladder, and announced to the occupants of the room that a few moons hence there would be a Masauû ceremony at Mastcomo.

At the departure of the dancers all occupants of the room crowded forward, each in turn placing his prayer symbol or feathered string in the basket tray, whispering a brief prayer to Masauû. This was an impressive ceremony, and was accompanied with much reverence. There was no loud talking, and each man seemed to speak confidentially to the personation of the supernatural being he addressed. Having received all the prayers of the kiva inmates, the two personations passed out of the room, leaving their trays full of stringed feathers. The situation of the shrines where these offerings were later placed was not observed, but some of them were placed at the shrine of Masauû in the foothills west of the mesa.

The foregoing rites and the nature of the prayers addressed to Masauû lead the author to regard him as a god of germination or a personation of fire as a symbol of life. Life, to a primitive mind, is power of will expressed in motion, and is the mystery which animates everything, organic and inorganic. Masauû has the mysterious power so developed that he can make crops grow if he wills, and he was appealed to for crops, as a germ god. There are other germ gods, as Muyiñwû or Alosaka, the germ god of Awatobi, but Masauû, one of the most archaic in Tusayan, was derived from Sikyatki. In early history, as legend declares, he owned all Hopi territory, but the chief of the Snake clan, by the use of his own mysterious power, overcame the mystery or medicine of Masauû, even though he had power of life and death, and compelled him to do good deeds.

Thus it is that Masauû is regarded as the god of fire, which is life; as the god of death; but above all as the god of germs, Eototo, whom the ancient Sikyatkians regarded as their special tutelary deity; once overcome by the Hopi, he now does their bidding.

APPEARANCE OF POWAMÛ KATCINAS

Certain beings called Powamû katcinas appear on the following morning in the kiva, where they dance and perform other rites. The artist has represented these, and also So wüqti (Grandmother woman), who grasps the Powamû katcina by the hand (see plate XIV).

DISTRIBUTION OF BEAN SPROUTS, DOLLS, AND OTHER OBJECTS

At sunrise of the last day of Powamû, two personations from each kiva distribute the sprouted beans, dolls, bows and arrows, moccasins, and other objects which have been made for that purpose. From their appearance at dawn they are called the Dawn (Telavai) katcinas, and in 1900 the following were observed performing this duty: Owa katcina, Malo katcina, Hehea katcina, Huhuan katcina, Sio Humis katcina, Tatcükti.

Shortly after this distribution a man personating Soyok wüqti went about Walpi holding conversations at the kivas and private houses, frightening children until they cried.

COLLECTION OF FOOD BY MONSTERS

Later in the day three groups of Soyoko or monsters, each group consisting of four Natackas, one Natacka mana, one Hahai wüqti, one Hehea katcina, and two Hehea katcina manas, went to every house of their pueblo demanding food from the inmates, as they had notified the people they would eight days previously. Hahai wüqti acted as speaker, assuming a falsetto voice, the Natackas emphasized the demands, and Hehea, armed with lassos, tried to rope those who refused. It is customary for the boys to first offer Hahai wüqti a mole or rat on a stick. This is refused, and then a small piece of meat, generally mutton, is held out. The Natacka examines it and if not large enough hands it back as he did the rat, shaking his hideous head. When the desired quantity of meat is presented, it is given to the Natacka mana, who transfers it to a basket she carries on her back. The girl or woman is then asked for meal, and she offers meal that she has ground from the ear of corn presented by the monsters on their previous visit. This is refused and more meal is demanded until enough is given to satisfy the monsters, who transfer it to the basket of Natacka mana, after which they retire.[a]

WINTER LAKONE PAHOLAWÜ

The Lalakontû have an assemblage in winter—a meeting of the chiefs, at which prayer sticks are made. This is held in Vensi's house near the Moñ kiva—the old house of the Patki clans. Vensi, the owner, is the oldest woman of the clan who is now active. No altar is put in place during this rite, which simply consists of prayers and songs.

---

[a] The monsters that visit the houses as described above are represented in a photograph taken at Walpi by Mr James Mooney and published with his permission in a paper in the Fifteenth Annual Report of the Bureau of American Ethnology, as plate cv. The names of these, beginning at the right of the line, are: 1, Hahai wüqti; 2, Natacka naamû; 3, Soyok mana; 4, Soyok mana; 5, 6, 7, 8, 9, Natackas of different-colored masks; 10, 11, 12, Heheas.

PALÜLÜKOÑTI, OR AÑKWAÑTI

This festival, like the two preceding, is an excellent one in which to study Hopi symbolism, for many masked personages appear in the dramatizations in the kivas and on the plazas outside. As has been shown elsewhere, the proceedings in the kivas are theatrical exhibitions which vary from year to year accordingly as one chief or another controls the different acts. Throughout the performance at which the author was present two old men, who may be called the kiva chiefs, sat by the fireplace in the middle of the room and continually fed the flames with small twigs of greasewood, the sole method of lighting the room on that night. The heat was very great and the ventilation was so poor that the atmosphere was stifling. The audience consisted mainly of women and children, who occupied one end of the room, the remainder being empty except while performances were being enacted. Everyone was gladly welcomed to see the performance, and there were probably not a dozen persons on the mesa who did not attend. No one paid admission to this theater and no actor received a recompense. It was a festival for all to enjoy, as all contributed to its success. Except in one act, no woman took part as an actor, and there were few men in the audience. The spectators assembled about 9 p. m., each clan seeking that kiva with which it had social affiliation. These acts are thus described in another paper:[a]

ACTS PERFORMED IN 1900

First Act

A voice was heard at the hatchway, as if someone were hooting outside, and a moment later a ball of meal, thrown into the room from without, landed on the floor by the fireplace. This was a signal that the first group of actors had arrived, and to this announcement the fire tenders responded, "Yuñya ai" ("Come in"), an invitation which was repeated by several of the spectators. After considerable hesitation on the part of the visitors and renewed cries to enter from those in the room, there was a movement above and the hatchway was darkened by the form of a man descending. The fire tenders rose and held their blankets about the fire to darken the room. Immediately there came down the ladder a procession of masked men bearing long poles, upon which was rolled a cloth screen, while under their blankets certain objects were concealed. Filing to the unoccupied end of the kiva, they rapidly set up the objects they bore. When they were ready a signal was given, and the fire tenders, dropping their blankets, resumed their seats by the fireplace. On the floor before our astonished eyes we saw a miniature field of corn, made of small clay pedestals out of which projected corn sprouts a few inches high. Behind

---

[a] A theatrical performance at Walpi, in Proceedings of the Washington Academy of Sciences, vol. II, Washington, 1900, pp. 607-626.

this field of corn hung a decorated cloth screen reaching from one wall of the room to the other and from the floor almost to the rafters. On this screen were painted many strange devices, among which were pictures of human beings, male and female, and of birds, symbols of rain clouds, lightning, and falling rain. Prominent among the symbols was a row of six circular disks, the borders of which were made of plaited corn husks, while the inclosed field of each was decorated with a symbolic picture of the sun. Men wearing grotesque masks[a] and ceremonial kilts stood on each side of this screen, one dressed as a woman and bearing in one hand a basket tray of meal and in the other an ear of corn. He wore a helmet with a coil of hair suspended on each side of the face, a bunch of feathers on the top, and a bang made of red horsehair hanging before the face. The helmet was painted black, and small crescents indicated the eyes and the mouth.

The act began with a song, to which the masked men, except the last-mentioned, danced. A hoarse roar made by a concealed actor blowing through an empty gourd[b] resounded from behind the screen, and immediately the circular disks swung open upward, and were seen to be flaps hinged above, covering orifices through which simultaneously protruded six artificial heads of serpents, realistically painted. Each head had protuberant goggle-eyes and bore a curved horn and a fan-like crest of hawk feathers. A mouth with teeth was cut in one end, and from this orifice there hung a strip of leather painted red, representing the tongue.

Slowly at first, but afterward more rapidly, these effigies were thrust farther into view, each revealing a body 4 or 5 feet long, painted, like the head, black on the back and white on the belly. When they were fully extended, the song grew louder, and the effigies moved back and forth, raising and depressing their heads in time, wagging them to one side or the other in unison. They seemed to bite ferociously at each other, and viciously darted at men standing near the screen. This remarkable play continued for some time, when suddenly the heads of the serpents bent down to the floor and swept across the imitation cornfield, knocking over the clay pedestals and the corn leaves which they supported. Then the effigies raised their heads and wagged them back and forth as before. It was observed that the largest effigy, that in the middle, had several udders on each side of the belly, and that she apparently suckled the others. Meanwhile the roar emitted from behind the screen by a concealed man continued, and wild excitement seemed to prevail. Some of the spectators threw meal at the effigies, offering prayers, amid shouts from others. The masked man representing a woman stepped forward and presented the contents of the basket tray to the serpent

---

a Representing the Bear katcinas.
b This gourd was decorated with the symbolic masks of the Great Plumed Snake.

effigies for food, after which he held his breasts to them as if to suckle them.[a]

Shortly after this the song diminished in volume, the effigies were slowly drawn back through the openings, the flaps on which the sun symbols were painted fell back into place, and after one final roar, made by the man behind the screen, the room was again silent. The overturned pedestals, with their corn leaves, were distributed among the spectators, and the two men by the fireplace again held up their blankets before the fire, while the screen was silently rolled up, and the actors with their paraphernalia departed.

The accompanying plate[b] represents the cloth screen tied in position to the roof of the kiva and the miniature cornfield on the floor before it. The six openings in the screen, four of which are larger than the other two, are arranged in a row, and out of five of these openings protrude serpent effigies. The flaps which ordinarily cover these orifices are raised, with the exception of that at the extreme right, which hangs in place to show the sun symbol on its face and the tip of a serpent's head near one margin. The central effigy (yuamû, their mother) is knocking over the rows of clay pedestals which form the miniature cornfield. The masked human figure standing at the left before the screen represents the mother of the clan gods, or Hahai wüqti, who is holding forward a basket tray of meal, which she offers as food to the serpents. One of the performers may be obscurely seen behind the screen, blowing the gourd trumpet by which the "roars" of the great serpents are imitated.

Prominent among the designs painted on this screen are three human figures. That of a man has two horns on the head like an Alosaka[c] and, as so often occurs in pictures or images on altars, the maidens have their hair arranged in disks, one above each ear, as in the Hopi maid's coiffure of the present day. These maidens were called Tubêboli manas. The other design represents birds, lightning, rain clouds, and falling rain. The first act was performed by men of the kiva which is situated in the middle of the Hano plaza,[d] and the screen and snake effigies are owned by men of that pueblo. The screen was repainted on the day of the dramatization by the men who took part in the act. No actor tasted food on that day before the decoration of the screen was finished, and at the close of their work all vomited over the cliffs. This Hano screen and the drama acted before it resemble those which are occasionally used in the chief kiva of Walpi.

---

[a] This actor represented Hahai wüqti, mother of katcinas or clan-ancients.
[b] Plate XXXII, Proc. Wash. Acad. Sci., vol. II, 1900.
[c] One of the prominent gods in Hopi worship.
[d] Called the Kisombi kiva, plaza kiva.

Second Act

The second act, a buffalo dance, was one of the best on this eventful night. Several men wearing helmets representing buffalo heads, with lateral horns and shaggy sheepskins, and wool painted black hanging down their backs, entered the room. They carried zigzag slats of wood, symbolic of lightning, and performed a characteristic dance to the beat of a drum. These buffalo personations were accompanied by a masked man and boy representing eagles, who danced before them, uttering calls in imitation of birds.

The same buffalo dance, but more complicated, was celebrated earlier in the winter in the public plaza of Walpi, at which time the men were accompanied by girls dressed as Buffalo maids who did not appear in the second act in the kivas. No representation of the eagles was seen in this public dance.

The Buffalo maids bore disks decorated with sun emblems on their backs, and carried notched sticks representing "sun ladders"[a] in their hands. It is appropriate that this dance should be given by men from the Tanoan pueblo, Hano, as it was probably introduced by men of the same stock from the Rio Grande region, by whom this village was settled.

Third Act

A new set of actors made their presence known at the entrance to the kiva soon after the departure of the Buffaloes, but these were found, on their entrance, to be very unlike those who had preceded them. They brought no sun screens nor serpent effigies with them, but were clothed in ceremonial kilts, and wore masks shaped like helmets. They were called Püükoñ katcinas, and were accompanied by two men dressed like women, one representing their grandmother and the other their mother. The former personated Kokyan wüqti,[b] or Spider woman, and wore a closely fitting mask with white crescentic eyes painted on a blackened face, and white hair made of raw cotton. She danced before the fire in the middle of the room, gracefully posturing her body and arms, while the others sang and danced to the beat of a drum. As the actors filed out of the room Spider woman distributed to the spectators seeds of corn, melon, and the like.[c]

---

[a] Ancient Hopi ladders were notched logs, some of which are still extant on the East mesa. In the winter solstice ceremony at Hano there stand, back of the altars, notched slats of wood called "sun ladders," which are supposed to be efficacious in rites recalling the sun or aiding an enfeebled sun to rise out of his "home." The prayer-sticks carried by the Buffalo maids are imitations of these sun ladders.

[b] This part was taken by Nanahe, a Hopi who has for many years made his home at Zuñi and returned to Walpi to be present at the dance.

[c] The mother and grandmother of Püükoñ katcinas naturally appear as representatives of the ancients of some clan with which this special form of the katcina cult originated. Hahai wüqti, who does not appear in this act, but in the first and fifth, is represented by Kokyan wüqti, probably the same supernatural under a different name.

Fourth Act

After the audience had sat silent for about a quarter of an hour men were heard walking on the roof and strange cries came down the hatchway. Again the fire tenders called to the visitors to enter, and muffled responses, as of masked persons outside, were heard in reply. First came down the ladder a man wearing a shabby mask covered with vertical zigzag lines,[a] bearing a heavy bundle on his back. As he climbed down the ladder he pretended to slip on each rung, but ultimately landed on the floor without accident, and opened his bundle, which was found to contain a metate and meal-grinding stone. He arranged these on the floor before the fireplace and took his place at one side. A second man with a like bundle followed, and deposited his burden by the side of tne other. Two masked girls,[b] elaborately dressed in white ceremonial blankets, followed, and knelt by the stones facing the fire, assuming the posture of girls when grinding corn.

After them entered the chorus, a procession of masked men who filed around the room and halted in line behind the kneeling girls. At a signal these last arrivals began to sing, and as they sang moved in a solemn dance. The girls rubbed the mealing stones back and forth over the metates, grinding the meal in time with the song, and the men clapped their hands, swaying their bodies in rhythm.

The last-mentioned men held an animated conversation with the fire tenders, asserting that the girls were expert meal grinders, and from time to time crossed the room, putting pinches of the meal into the mouths of the fire tenders and spectators. This continued for some time, after which the girls rose and danced in the middle of the room, posturing their bodies and extending alternately their hands, in which they carried corn ears. The chorus personated the Navaho Añya katcinas, the girls were called the Navaho Añya maids and were supposed to be sisters of men in the chorus.

In order better to understand this act, let us consider the nature of the cult from which the personages appearing in it were derived. These personages are called katcinas, of which there are many kinds among the Hopis, differing from each other in the symbolism of their masks and other paraphernalia. Their distinctive names are totemistic, the same as those of clans now living either at Walpi or at some other place from which the katcinas were derived. Katcinas are tutelary clan gods of the ancestral type, and when personated appear as both males and females.

In many cases the katcina is represented by no clan of the same totemistic name now living in the pueblo. This has been brought about in several ways, of which there may be mentioned: (1) The

---

[a] These men were called Hehea katcinas.

[b] These girls were called the Tacab Añya katcina manas. On the day following, two girls representing the Añya katcina manas performed the same act in the public plaza of Walpi.

clan has become extinct, while its katcina has survived; (2) a katcina has been purchased or borrowed from a neighboring people; (3) a katcina mask has been invented by some imaginative person who has seen an object which he thinks fitting for a katcina totem.

A study of a clan and the katcina which bears the same name will be instructive in the determination of their relation.

There are several clans where this clan relation of the katcina still retains its primitive totemistic character, and at least one where the names of both clan and katcina are the same. For instance, the members of the Tcakwaina or Asa clans claim that the Tcakwaina katcinas are their clan-ancients, and when they personate these clan-ancients they represent the following masked personages:

1. Tcatcakwaina taamû,	Tcakwainas, their uncle.	
2. Tcatcakwaina tatakti,	Tcakwainas, males (brothers).	
3. Tcatcakwaina kokoiamû,	Tcakwainas, their elder sister.	
4. Tcatcakwaina mamantû (=manas),	Tcakwainas, maids (sisters).	
5. Tcatcakwaina yuamû,	Tcakwainas, their mother.	

It will be noticed that all these ancestral personages belong to one and the same clan—the mother, brothers (tatakti), sisters (mamanantû), and uncle—but that the father is unrepresented.

The most important fact, however, is that the name of the katcinas is the same as that of the clan, viz., Tcakwaina, and that men of this clan personate in dramatic and ceremonial performances the supernaturals bearing their clan name. They do not introduce a personation of the Tcakwaina father because he is not of their clan, and hence can not be a supernatural of their clan.

An analysis of other katcinas shows that many of them are ancients of clans, or that each clan originally had distinctive divinized ancients in the katcina cult. These gods are personated as brothers, sisters, uncle, mother, or grandmother, the paraphernalia being determined by the particular clan totem.

The relation of a katcina to its clan can be traced in many other instances, but in others, and perhaps the majority, it is obscured by changes in nomenclature and sociologic development. Katcinas often no longer bear their ancient names, but are called from some peculiarity of dress, prominent symbol of the mask, or peculiar cry emitted by them, which has no connection with the totems of their respective clans. The Añya katcinas (brothers, men) and the Añya katcina manas (sisters) belong to this group. They were originally introduced by Patki (Rain-cloud clans) from settlements on the Little Colorado river, and their name has no relation to the clans which brought them. In fact at Zuñi the dance of these katcinas is called the Kokshi, Good dance, while the name of the same at Walpi is the Añya, or Long-hair. We have also at the latter pueblos other names for the Añya manas, as Soyal manas, equally inapplicable so far as their clan relation is concerned.

The popular names of Hopi gods, among which are included katcinas or clan tutelary supernaturals, are commonly of exoteric origin and are oftentimes very numerous. Unfortunately the archaic name is often lost, although in a few cases it is the same as the popular.

Fifth Act

As after former acts, we waited a few minutes only for the next, a fifth, which was somewhat similar in character to the first. A call at the hatchway and an invitation from within to enter led to the appearance of a procession of masked men who came down the ladder bearing paraphernalia for their exhibition hidden under their arms or concealed in blankets. The fire tenders shielded the fire once more with blankets, so that the room was darkened, and in the obscure light the actors arranged their stage properties. When the blankets were dropped, the light revealed on the floor before us an imitation field of corn, each hill of which was a clay pedestal with projecting corn leaves, and behind it, as a background, a wooden framework decorated with peripheral turkey feathers [a] and hung with two disks painted with sun emblems. Pine boughs were so arranged in the framework that they filled all vacant spaces and shielded performers in the rear of the room. Several naked men, called "mudheads," wearing on their heads close-fitting cloth bags with attached knobs, stood before the framework, which was supported by two of their number. The exercises opened with "roars" from behind the disks and vigorous dancing by the mudheads before the screen.

Soon the flaps of the sun disks swung open and from under them emerged the hideous heads of two snake effigies, larger than those of the first performance, but similarly constructed. These serpent heads were thrust forward until their serpentine bodies, extended several feet, came into view. Their heads darted back and forth, swaying first to one side and then to the other, biting viciously now at the audience and then at each other, while deep roars imitating the voice of the serpent emerged from the rear of the room. With one stroke of the head the field of corn was swept over and the serpents twisted their bodies about each other.

One of the naked men, a mudhead, wearing the knobbed cloth bag, stepped forward and grasped one of the serpent effigies by the neck. He pretended to wrestle with the snake, and for a time was successful, but at last the man was overcome and sent sprawling on the floor. Then another advanced to the conflict, and he too was thrown down. A youthful mudhead made a like attempt and mounted the effigy, riding on its neck as if on horseback. The whole act was a realistic representation of the struggle of man with the serpent. Ultimately the serpents contracted their bodies, drew back

---

[a] Sun shields commonly have eagle feathers inserted about their borders.

their heads behind the flaps, and the performance ended with a prolonged roar from behind the screen. In the darkness which followed, made by hanging blankets before the fire, the actors packed their paraphernalia, gathered their effigies, and quietly left the room.

The accompanying plate[a] represents this fifth act, or the struggle of the mudhead with the serpent effigies. The framework, which is supported by two men, is decorated with zigzag symbols representing lightning; the row of semicircular bodies on the crossbeam symbolizes the rain clouds, from which descend parallel marks, the falling rain. These six semicircular rain-cloud symbols are of different colors, yellow, green, red, and white, corresponding to the supposed colors of the cardinal points, and all have animal designs representing frogs and birds painted upon them. The manipulators of the serpent effigies are hidden from view by pine or cedar boughs inserted into a log on the floor, which is covered with figures of rings, symbolic of the earth. At the right of a median vertical line a serpent effigy is seen protruded through an opening, above which is a circular flap raised to a horizontal position. The serpent effigy on this side is searching for a youthful "mudhead," who has crawled below the disk. The left-hand serpent is represented in conflict with an adult mudhead, who has grasped it about the body and neck; the serpent appears to be biting at its opponent. We are looking at this strange contest from the raised spectators' floor of the kiva; the miniature cornfield, which one of the serpents knocked down a short time before, has been removed, and the clay pedestals which remained are distributed among the spectators. The weird effects of the light from the fireplace in the middle of the room have been brought out by the artist, Mrs Gill, who has successfully drawn these screens from the author's kodak photographs and sketches.

Sixth Act

There was yet another exhibition of serpent effigies in this continuous performance, and the actors were announced in much the same way as their predecessors. They appeared shortly after the departure of the Spider woman and her associates, and arranged their paraphernalia in the darkened room, holding up an additional blanket to conceal their preparations. When the blankets were dropped from before the fire, a miniature field of corn was seen on the kiva floor, and back of it were two vases surrounded, except on the side toward the fire, by a row of squatting mudheads. A song immediately began, and suddenly the four lappets [b] which covered the orifice of each vase were turned back automatically, when out of the vases slowly

---

[a] Plate XXXIII, Proc. Wash. Acad. Sci., vol. II, 1900.

[b] These four semicircular flaps, symbols of rain clouds, were painted in four colors, yellow, green, red, and white. On the necks of the vases were parallel lines, symbols of falling rain, and on their sides were stars and tadpole decoration. Each vase was placed on a bed of cedar or pine boughs to make it more stable.

emerged the heads of two artificial serpents drawing their bodies behind them. These effects were produced by hidden strings placed over the kiva rafters, and the images were made by this means to rise and fall, move backward and forward, or to approach each other. Their heads were drawn down to the floor and swept over the miniature cornfield, overturning it as in the first act, when a sun screen was also employed. They struggled with each other, winding their heads together, and performed various other gyrations at the wish of the manipulators. The effects produced with these strings were effective, and the motions of the men who held the strings and manipulated the effigies were closely concealed. It is probable that some of the strings were attached to the rattles used by the chorus.

The performance was a very realistic one, for in the dim light of the room the strings were invisible, and the serpents seemed to rise voluntarily from the vases. At its close the effigies sank into the cavities of the vases and the song ceased. In the darkness the paraphernalia were wrapped in blankets, and the actors left the room, passing to another kiva, where the performance was repeated. The personators of this act were from the Tcivato kiva of Walpi, and their chief was Pautiwa.

While we were witnessing these six exhibitions in one room shows were simultaneously being enacted in the other eight kivas on the East mesa. The six sets of actors, each with their paraphernalia, passed in turn from one room to another, in all of which spectators awaited their coming. Each of the performances was given nine times that night, and it may safely be said that all were witnessed by the 500 people who comprise the population of the three pueblos in one kiva or another.[a] It was midnight when this primitive theater closed, and the effigies were disjointed and carried to hidden crypts in the houses, where they were luted in jars with clay, not to see the light again until March of the next year.

ADDITIONAL ACTS SOMETIMES PERFORMED

Although the sixth act closed the series of theatrical exhibitions in 1900, it by no means exhausts the dramatic resources of the Hopis in the presentation of their Great Serpent exhibition. This year (1900) was said by all to be one of abbreviation in all winter ceremonies and dramatic performances, but in more elaborate exhibitions, in other years, instead of six there are, we are told, as many as nine acts in this continuous show, employing one set of actors from each kiva on the mesa. Our account would be more comprehensive if it included short references to one or two of the important additional acts which occur in the more elaborate performance.[b]

---

[a] On such occasions each clan assembles in a certain kiva, which is said to be the kiva of that clan.

[b] The sun screen and serpent effigies used by men of the Nacab kiva have been described in a former article (The Palülükoñti, Journal of American Folk-Lore, vol. II, 1893). This performance has many points of likeness to that of actors from the plaza kiva of Hano, described in the first act.

Sometimes the screen performance is accompanied by an exhibition by a masked man or men, who pretend to struggle with a snake effigy which they carry in their arms. This performance consists mainly in twisting these effigies about the body and neck of the performer, holding them aloft, or even throwing them to the roof of the kiva, as elsewhere [a] described in an account of the celebration in 1893.

In some years marionettes representing Corn maids are substituted for the two masked girls in the act of grinding corn, and these two figures are very skillfully manipulated by concealed actors. Although this representation was not introduced in 1900, it has often been described to me, and one of the Hopi men has drawn me a picture of the marionettes, which is worth reproduction in a plate (see plate XXVII).

The figurines are brought into a darkened room wrapped in blankets, and are set up near the middle of the kiva in much the same way as the screens. The kneeling images, surrounded by a wooden framework, are manipulated by concealed men; when the song begins they are made to bend their bodies backward and forward in time, grinding the meal on miniature metates before them. The movements of girls in grinding meal are so cleverly imitated that the figurines, moved by hidden strings, at times raise their hands to their faces, which they rub with meal as the girls do when using the grinding stones in their rooms.

During this marionette performance two bird effigies were made to walk back and forth along the upper horizontal bar of the framework, while bird calls issued from the rear of the room.

The substitution of marionettes for masked girls suggests an explanation of the use of idols among the Hopis. A supernatural being of the Hopi Olympus may be represented in ceremony or drama by a man wearing a mask, or by a graven image or picture, a symbol of the same. Sometimes one, sometimes the other method of representing the god is employed, and often both. The image may be used on the altar, while the masked man appears in the public exhibition in the pueblo plaza. Neither idol nor masked personators are worshipped, but both are regarded as symbolic representations in which possibly the gods may temporarily reside.

So with the use of marionettes to represent the Corn maidens in the theatrical exhibition or the personation of the beings by masked girls. They are symbolic representations of the mythic maidens whose beneficent gifts of corn and other seeds in ancient times is a constant theme in Hopi legends.

The clan ancients or katcinas personated in the Great Serpent drama vary from year to year, implying the theatrical nature of the festival, but there are certain of these personations which invariably

---

[a] Article cited. The masked man who thus struggles with the serpent effigy represents Calako, a sun god, but figures of him drawn by a Hopi artist were called Macibol katcina.

appear. In the exhibition of 1893, the only one previous to 1900 on which we have reliable notes, there was one performance with a sun screen and serpent effigies which were manipulated by the men of the kiva under the Snake rock. The symbols depicted on this screen differed somewhat from those on the screen employed in 1900, but the general character of the performance with it was the same. Briefly considered the acts given in 1893 were as follow:

First act. An exhibition with the sun screen and serpent effigies by men of Nacab kiva similar to the first act of 1900, but in which the actors personated Pawik (Duck), Tacab (Navaho), Hahai wüqti, and others. A masked man (Calako) stood before the screen holding in his arms an effigy of a Great Snake with which he appeared to struggle, and for that reason was called "The Struggling One." The serpent effigy carried was manipulated in such a way that the man and snake appeared to be engaged in a combat, much as in the fifth act of 1900, except that the serpent effigy was not thrown through an opening closed by a disk bearing sun symbols. The manipulator wore a false arm[a] hanging from one shoulder in place of his real arm, which was thrust within the body of the effigy, grasping a stick, the "backbone" of the monster.

Second act. Dance of masked men representing Añya katcinas.

Third act. Dance of masked men representing Tacab katcinas.

Fourth act. Dance of masked men representing clowns and two Huhuan katcinas.

Fifth act. Dance of men personating women of the Owakültû society, who threw their baskets to the spectators.

Sixth act. Dance of men representing old women bearing willow wands.

Seventh act. Dance of masked men representing Tanoan Añya katcinas.

The god of death, Masauû,[b] was personated in the 1893 exhibition and appeared in the plaza about 2 p. m., "dancing through Walpi with a hobbling movement, singing snatches of a song. He was masked and wrapped in a rabbit-skin rug, and went to all the kivas, beating the entrance with a bush" (*Bigelovia graveolens*).

On the day following the night exhibition in 1893 there were public dances of the Tacab and Añya katcinas.

PARAPHERNALIA USED, THEIR CONSTRUCTION AND SYMBOLISM

The effigies of Palülükoñ now used at the East mesa are not very ancient, although there are one or two which show considerable antiquity. One of these older specimens has a body of buckskin, but the majority, and all the recent ones, are made of cotton cloth. The

---

a For figures of the false arm see Journal of American Folk-Lore, vol. VI, 1893, plate II.

b Two boys took this part in 1900.

present screens are of the latter material, but these are commonly said to have replaced others of skin or native cloth. The Walpi men made two new serpent effigies in their kivas in 1900, and all the material of which they were manufactured was purchased from the neighboring trader at Keams Canyon.

Each of the three pueblos, Hano, Sichumovi, and Walpi, has several of these serpent effigies, which are kept in the houses of the following clans:

Hano, Sa (Tobacco) clan; Sichumovi, Patki (Rain-cloud) clan; Walpi, Tcüa (Snake) clan, Pakab (Reed) clan.

In ancient times they were kept in stone inclosures outside the pueblos, but these receptacles have been abandoned of late, on account of the inroads of nomads. It is said that the Oraibi and Middle mesa pueblos still have extramural receptacles for the Palülükoñ effigies. The house of the ancient Plumed Snake of Hano is a small cave in the side of the mesa near the ruin Türkinobi, where several broken serpent heads and effigy ribs, or wooden hoops, can now be seen, although the entrance is walled up and rarely opened.

A knowledge of the mechanical construction of the serpent effigies may aid in an understanding of their manipulation. Their heads are either cut out of cottonwood or made of gourds, and are painted, and the protuberant goggle-eyes are small buckskin bags tied to the top. Each head bears a medial horn curving forward, sometimes made with joints and at other times solid. A radiating crest of hawk feathers is tied vertically to the back of the head. The teeth are cut in the gourd or wood of which the head is made and are painted red. The tongue is a leather strap, also painted red, and protrudes from the mouth a considerable distance. The top of the head is black, the bottom white, and these same colors continue along the sides of the body.

The body consists of a central stick, called a backbone, over which is extended a covering that is held in place by a series of hoops graduated in size from the neck to the end. The effigy is manipulated by means of a stick, held by a man behind the screen. The "backbone" has a ferule cut in it a few inches back of the neck, and to this ferule are tied a quartz crystal called the heart and a package which contains corn seeds of all colors, melon, squash, cotton, and other seeds, and a black prayer-stick. The cotton cloth stretched over the series of hoops, called ribs, which form the body, is painted black above and white below, with a red streak at the dividing line, where there are also other markings and symbols, like those on the kilts of the Snake priests.

The backbones of the two effigies which were made to rise out of the vases were short and stumpy, but they have a "heart" similar to the longer ones, and an attached package of seeds.

RÉSUMÉ OF EVENTS IN PALÜLÜKOÑTI IN 1900

February 14. On this day corn was planted in three kivas, the Moñ kiva, Tcivato kiva of Walpi, and the plaza kiva of Hano. This corn was daily watered and the kivas were heated so that the seeds might sprout. The miniature cornfield was later made of these sprouts. Children are not allowed to know that the corn is thus planted before the exhibition. The planting of corn seeds has given the name "Corn planting" to Palülükoñti, just as the one of beans in a like way gave the name "Bean planting" to the Powamû, but these names characterize incidents not the true purpose of the festival.

February 26. About two weeks after the corn seeds were planted the effigies of the Great Serpent were brought into the three kivas above mentioned at nightfall, when the rehearsals of the acts to be given later took place.

February 27 (Yuñya). This day was devoted to the preparation of the paraphernalia, and at sundown there was a rehearsal of the Great Serpent acts, as also on the following day.

March 1 (Komoktotokya). In addition to the rehearsals in the kiva, masked men representing Wupamau, Honau, Hehea, Mucaias, Wuyok, Soyan ep, and Samo wüqtaka katcinas appeared in the plazas. They dressed and masked themselves at Wala (The Gap), and marched up the trail into Hano, where they gathered at the kiva hatches, and held an animated conversation with the chief of the kiva, who came to the hatchway for that purpose.

March 2 (Totokya). Many masked men were seen throughout the day in the three East mesa pueblos. Early in the afternoon there were noticed in Hano three Woe katcinas, each with a chevron mark on the face, and one Wupamau, or Big High Sky god, bearing the sun mask[a], and held by a mudhead priest by a rope tied about his loins. In Walpi shortly afterward two small boys dressed and masked to represent Masauû went from one kiva to another, standing on the hatch and beating the ladder with bundles of sticks.

Late in the afternoon the chief kiva of Hano sent to all the kivas on the East mesa a delegation of masked men representing Mucaias, Buffalo; Wupamau, Big High Sky (sun) god; Honau, Bear; Ahote; Citoto; Tcanaû; Wukokoti; and many mudheads. They went from one kiva entrance to another, holding conversations with the kiva chiefs and in various ways amusing the spectators.

About sundown the men of the two Walpi kivas carried their snake effigies to the main spring of the pueblo, the home of Palülükoñ, called Tawapa, Sun spring, where they performed ceremonies, while the men of Hano took their serpent effigies to a spring called

---

[a] The symbols of this mask resemble those of Tawa (sun) disks, and those of the masks of Ahül, Ahülani, and Wüwtiyomo, showing that the latter are probably the same sun gods under different clan names.

Moñwiva, sacred to their Great Snake. The six acts in the kivas were performed directly after the return of the men with the effigies from these springs.

During the festival all actors abstain from salt and meat and do not sleep with their wives, a tabu which is rigidly observed, especially on the day preceding the exhibition in the kiva.

On several of the days of this festival there are foot races along the water courses in the valley, during which the naked racers kick small stone nodules in a sinistral circuit around the mesa. This was a prayer for streams full of water.

The events which occurred when the effigies were taken to the springs were wholly ceremonial, and not dramatic. During the day previous to this event, all men of prominence, especially chiefs of clans, brought feathered strings to the kivas, and tied them to the necks of the serpent effigies. One or more prayer-sticks were also made to be used at the springs. Six of these were made in the performance of 1893. One was tied to the backbone of each effigy. Five others were deposited at the spring, some at the edge of the water, others beneath it.

The exercises at the springs Tawapa and Moñwiva were not witnessed by the author in 1900, but they were probably the same as were described in the account of this episode in 1893.[a] In that year, about 7.30 p. m., a procession went down to the spring carrying the effigies and the trumpets by which the roars of the serpent are imitated. This procession was led by a man personating Hahai wüqti and the kiva chief, "making a connecting trail from the south edge of the basin [Tawapa], along the east and north sides of the pool, and up as close to the west edge as the mud would permit. Those following with the serpent effigies, beginning at the east side of the pool, laid the effigies down close to the edge of the water, along the north side. The youths placed their gourd trumpets on the meal trail, upon which also were the serpent effigies. All then sat on the north side facing the south. The leader, as he went down, deposited the five pahos . . . at the west side of the pool, setting them in a row fronting the east.

"The leader of the procession bore the kopitcoki (cedar bark slow match). . . . It had been lighted at the kiva fire before the procession started, and the fire was smouldering in the bark. Momi (kiva chief) lit a pipe by this torch and gave it to the leader, who made the usual response, smoked a few puffs and passed it to the next man on his right. Momi then lit another pipe and passed it also to the leader, and the two pipes passed down the two lines, in which they had arranged themselves when sitting, the elders in front, next the pool, the youths behind them. After all had smoked, the leader prayed, and each of the nine elders followed in succession. The ten youths did not pray, but each took his trumpet [gourd] and, stepping one stride into the pool, stooped over, and, placing the bulbous end to his mouth with the small orifice on the surface of the water, trumpeted three or four times. Each of the youths then dipped up a little water in his trumpet and poured it into a vase.

"The effigy bearers then dipped the tip of the serpents' heads and the ends of the hawk-tail plumes in the pool, and the leader said a short prayer and started back up the trail."

Certainly the most remarkable of all the masked men who appeared that day were the two personations of a being called Tcanaû katcina. They wore circular masks with feathers projecting from the periphery and carried in their mouths realistic stuffed effigies of rattlesnakes, while over the eyes of the masks were fastened carved wooden effigies of lizards. Although these masks suggest the custom of the well-known Snake dance, not the Snake clan but the Pakab clan is said to have introduced this ceremony into the Walpi ferial calendar.

March 3 (Tihüni). On the day after the acts in the kivas there was a public dance of the Añya katcinas in the Walpi plaza. During this dance grinding stones were placed in the middle of the open space by the Snake rock, behind which two girls representing Añya katcina manas took their position, and a line of Añya katcinas extended the whole length of the plaza. The latter served as chorus, while the girls ground meal, as in a kiva performance the night before.

In this exhibition or dance there were also two men personating Hehea, whose actions were identical with those of the same personations in the kiva performance. They sat on the ground as the girls ground the meal and the chorus sang. The personators in this dance were from the chief kiva of Walpi, and the exhibition has the same meaning as that of the night before.

There also appeared in this public exhibition a masked personage called Hopak (Eastern) katcina, the signification of whose presence is unknown to the author.

PERSONATIONS APPEARING IN PALÜLÜKOÑTI

The following personations appear in Palülükoñti:

Woe (Eagle). Appears in kiva drama.
Wupamau. Wanders through the pueblos, accompanied by a mudhead, who lassoes whomever he meets.
Honau (Bear). Appears in kiva drama.
Ahote. Wanders through the pueblo.
Citoto. Appears in public with other masked men.
Tcanaû. Appears with preceding.
Wukokoti. Appears with preceding.
Kwahu (Eagle). Appears in kiva drama.
Püükoñ (War god). Appears in kiva drama.

Kokyan wüqti. Appears in kiva drama.
Püükoñ's sister. Appears in kiva drama.
Tacab Añya. Appears in kiva drama.
Tacab Añya mana. Appears in kiva drama.
Hahai wüqti. Appears in kiva drama.
Añya. Performs ceremonial dance in plaza.
Añya mana. Grinds corn in ceremonial dance in plaza.
Hehea. Appears in ceremonial dance in plaza.
Hopak. Appears in ceremonial dance in plaza.

Winter Marau Paholawû

The winter prayer-stick-making of the Mamzrautû society was much more complicated in 1900 than that of the Lalakoñtû. The row of upright objects from the altar erected in October was put in place and before it were laid the tiponis of the chiefs of the society. On the final day there was a public dance in which there were personations of the Palahiko manas. The Hopi artist has made a fair picture of one of these Palahiko manas, which is here reproduced in plate LVI.

Spring Sumaikoli

The Yaya priests and Sumaikoli hold a spring festival in Walpi, which in some particulars resembles the Sumaikoli celebration at Hano, elsewhere described.[a]

The six masks of Sumaikoli and one of Kawikoli are arranged on the floor of the kiva behind the tiponis. New fire is kindled with rotating fire drills, and this fire is later carried by means of cedar-bark torches to shrines of the Fire god, four shrines in the foothills, where bonfires are kindled in sequence, north, west, south, and east.

The carriers who bear these torches, and who kindle the four fires, deposit in the contiguous shrines prayer-sticks which have been made in the kiva before their exit.

One of the most interesting features in the songs which are sung before the altar are the calls down a hole in the floor called the sipapû to the goddess of the earth.[b] This being is represented by a bundle of sticks placed on the floor, and over this bundle the priest kneels when he shouts to the earth goddess.

The symbolism of the Sumaikoli masks at Walpi is similar to that of the Hano masks, which are elsewhere[c] figured and described. They differ among themselves mainly in the colors of the different symbols. The picture of the Sumaikoli by the Hopi artist (see plate xxxiv) gives a fair idea of the paraphernalia.

---

[a] Journal of American Ethnology and Archæology, vol. ii, 1892.

[b] See The Lesser New-Fire Ceremony at Walpi, American Anthropologist, new series, vol. iii, July–September, 1901.

[c] Journal of American Ethnology and Archæology, vol. ii, 1892. In this early description these objects were erroneously called shields. They are worn before the face in elaborate Sumaikoli celebrations.

Abbreviated Katcina Dances

Throughout the summer months there occur in the Hopi pueblos a series of masked dances, generally of a day's duration, to which the author has given the name Abbreviated Katcina dances. They are not accompanied by secret ceremonies, and the participants vary in number, the beings personated differing from year to year.

These dances close with what is called the Niman, or Departure of the Katcinas, a ceremony of nine days' duration, in which there is an elaborate altar, and many secret ceremonies.[a] There are, however, no altars in these abbreviated festivals, nor is there any public announcement of them by the town crier. The dances continue at intervals from morning to night, but are limited to one day, the three or four preceding days being spent in the kivas practicing songs, preparing and painting dance paraphernalia, and making other preparations for the public exhibition. The katcinas in these festivals are accompanied by one or more unmasked priests, who shout to them, sprinkle the dancers with meal, and lead the line as it passes from one dance place to another, showing the trail by sprinkling meal on the ground. These are called the katcina fathers (naamû), and in a general way correspond to the rain priests mentioned by students of Zuñi ceremonies.

Ordinarily all participants in one of these abbreviated dances wear masks with like symbols, but there are four or six dressed as women who accompany the dance by rasping a sheep scapula on a notched stick. Occasionally, however, there is a dance, limited to one day, in which all participants wear different kinds of masks, and personate different katcinas. This dance, known as the Soyohim, has been elsewhere described.[b] From the variety of personations which appear, this dance is a particularly good one for a study of the Hopi symbolism.

Summer Tawa Paholawû (Sun Prayer-stick-making)

The making of the sun prayer-sticks in midsummer is limited to a single day, but does not differ from that in winter.[c] The Sun priests assemble for this purpose in the room under a house near the Moñ kiva, and the only fetish they use is a stone image of a frog, over which is stretched a string with attached feathers, and which lies on a line of meal drawn diagonally on the floor.

As the Sun priests have no distinctive masks or public dance, no pictures were made to illustrate this ceremony.

---

[a] For a description of Niman Katcina see Journal of American Ethnology and Archæology, vol. II, 1892, p. 86.

[b] Same volume, p. 59.

[c] The summer sun prayer-stick-making at both Walpi and Hano is described in the volume just cited.

Summer Sumaikoli

The summer Sumaikoli at Walpi has never been seen by an ethnologist, but the ceremony at Hano is elsewhere described.[a] It is a single day ceremony in which the seven Sumaikoli masks, to which the priests pray, are set in a row on a buckskin at one end of the room. Feathers (nakwakwoci) are tied to the masks (shields), and prayer-sticks are made and distributed to distant shrines.

The Sumaikoli helmet masks of Hano were captured in some Navaho foray and strewn about the base of the mesa. They were gathered by Kalacai, and are now kept with pious care in the room near Kalakwai's new house in Hano, where they can be seen hanging to the wall. With Kalacai's death the Sun clan (Tän towa) of Hano became extinct and the care of the Sumaikoli devolved on others.

There was no public exhibition of the Sumaikoli in the summer of 1891, but the author has been told that the festival has of late been revived in Hano. The Hopi artist has given a fairly good picture of Sumaikoli as he appears in public [b] (see plate XXXIV).

Niman

This is an elaborate festival celebrating the departure of the katcinas from Walpi, and consists of elaborate rites before a complicated altar and a public dance, which differs in different Hopi pueblos. One of these is described in another place.[c] This is the only festival celebrating the departure of the katcinas, although there are several commemorating their advent. Thus, the Soyaluña dramatizes the advent of the Water-house or Rain-cloud clan's katcinas, the Pamürti that of Zuñi clans, especially Asa and Honani, and the Powamû the advent of the ancients of the Katcina clans.

Tcüatikibi, Snake Dance

The Snake dance has no masked performers, and the artist has not drawn pictures of any of the participants.

Leleñti, or Leñpaki, Flute Dance

The Flute dance also has no masked personators, and the artist has furnished no picture of participants. It might have been well to have obtained pictures of the Flute girls and youth, but photographs have been published[d] which show their paraphernalia better than native pictures. The Snake girl is dressed almost identically as the Flute girl, as shown by the figures mentioned.

a Journal of American Ethnology and Archæology, vol. II, 1892, p. 33.

b Dellenbaugh has published a few cuts from photographs representing Sumaikoli personations, but the symbolism of the masks is not clearly indicated in them. See The North Americans of Yesterday, New York, 1901.

c Journal of American Ethnology and Archæology, vol. II, 1892, p. 79.

d Nineteenth Annual Report of the Bureau of American Ethnology, part II, 1900.

BULITIKIBI, BUTTERFLY DANCE

The Butterfly festival, which is occasionally celebrated in Sichumovi, differs from the Lalakoñti, Mamzrauti, and Owakülti by the absence of secret rites, altar, tiponi, or other fetishes. While these three festivals are nine days' long, with many elaborate secret rites, Bulitikibi is a one-day's public dance, without secret rites.

The artist has figured two Buli manas or Butterfly girls as they are dressed when taking part in this dance, and a leader bearing a pole with attached streamers (see plate LVII). Many men and girls participate in this dance, their dress and paraphernalia corresponding very closely with that of the Tablita dancers of the Rio Grande pueblos.

LALAKOÑTI

This festival is one of the most regular in the Hopi calendar, occurring each year in September. It is a woman's dance, with many secret rites, an elaborate altar, and a public exhibition, during which baskets and other objects are thrown to the assembled spectators. Most of the women who take part in this dance carry baskets, which they move in cadence with their songs. There are two maids called the Lakone girls, who throw the baskets and other objects to the spectators.

The Hopi artist has represented the latter dressed in their customary paraphernalia (plate LV), but there is a slight difference in the dress of these girls in the Lalakoñti at Walpi and at the other pueblos.[a]

OWAKÜLTI

This is likewise a woman's basket dance, which is occasionally celebrated at Sichumovi, but is not an annual festival at that pueblo. Like the Lalakoñti it has an elaborate altar which, however, differs very widely from that of other basket dances.

The Lalakoñti was introduced into Tusayan by the Patki or Raincloud clans; the Owakülti was brought from Awatobi by the Pakab and Buli clans.

MAMZRAUTI[b]

This festival is likewise a woman's dance, but the participants, instead of carrying baskets in their hands, as in the Lalakoñti and Owakülti, carry slats of wood bearing appropriate symbols.

Two girls called the Mamzrau manas (Mamzrau maids) appear in this dance, and throw objects on the ground. The Hopi artist has made two pictures of these girls, which show the style of their dress and paraphernalia (see plate LV).

---

[a] See article on the Lalakoñti, American Anthropologist, vol. V, 1892, p. 105.

[b] For description of Mamzrauti see American Anthropologist, July, 1892. Many ceremonies are named from the society which celebrates them and the termination pakit, to go down into the kiva; thus we have Maraupaki, Leñpaki, etc.

DESCRIPTION OF THE PICTURES

The symbolism of the different beings mentioned in the preceding pages may be sufficiently well made out by an examination of the following pictures and descriptions; but in order to facilitate references they are arranged, so far as possible, in the sequence in which the beings they represent appear in the Hopi ferial calendar. As the principal symbols are always delineated on the mask, special attention is given to the head in these descriptions. The words "head" and "mask" are used interchangeably.

The collection does not contain representations of all katcinas with which the Hopis are acquainted, nor is it claimed that pictures made by another man might not vary somewhat from those here figured. The chief symbolic designs characteristic of different gods are, however, brought out with such distinctness that all would be immediately recognized by any intelligent Hopi.

PAMÜRTI CEREMONY

PAUTIWA

(Plate II)*

The picture of the Zuñi[a] sun god, Pautiwa, has a horizontal dumb-bell-shaped design across a green face, and a long protuberant snout.[b] It has terraced symbols, representing rain clouds, attached to each side of the head, and a pine-bough collar tied around the neck. The head is crowned by a cluster of bright-colored feathers, and white cotton strings hang from the hair.

The figure carries a skin meal pouch and a wooden slat (moñkohû) in the left hand, and two crooked sticks in the right. The blankets, kilt, great cotton girdle, and other bodily paraphernalia are similar to those in other pictures.

From his preeminence in the Pamürti, Pautiwa[c] is evidently a very important god, and, although his objective symbolism is unlike that of other Hopi sun gods, the part he plays is so similar to that played by Ahül that he may be identified as a sun god. As the Hopi representation was derived from Zuñi, we may look to students of the mythology of that pueblo for an exact determination of his identity.

Pautiwa was a leader of the Pamürti at Sichumovi in 1900, and the part was taken by Homovi. The ceremony opened by Pautiwa, fully masked and dressed, going from kiva to kiva informing the men that a meeting would be held at Homovi's house on a certain date not

---

[a] The Zuñi name also is Pautiwa.

[b] For picture of the doll see Internationales Archiv für Ethnographie, Band VII, pl. VIII, fig. 23.

[c] The ending "tiwa" is common in Hopi personal names of men, as Intiwa, Masiumtiwa, and Wikyatiwa.

*Plate I pertains to the essay preceding Dr. Fewkes's article in the *Twenty-First Annual Report of the Bureau of American Ethnology to the Secretary of the Smithsonian Institution.*

many days distant. At each kiva Pautiwa unmasked and smoked with the kiva chiefs.

At the meeting it was decided what personations should appear in Pamürti and who should take part.

CIPIKNE

(Plate II)

Another Zuñi katcina who appears in the Pamürti is called Cipikne, a drawing of whom is here given. In the picture the color of the mask is yellow, and there is a protuberant snout painted blue. Across the face the painter has drawn a dumb-bell-shaped symbol colored black, with a red border, resembling a like design in the Pautiwa figure. On the head there is depicted a bundle of feathers, and a collar made of the same objects is represented about the neck.

The symbolism of Cipikne resembles that of Zuñi beings called Salamopias,[a] with which he would seem to be identical. In the festival mentioned the Hopis personated two Cipiknes, differing only in color. The Zuñis are said to be acquainted with several Salamopias of different colors.

HAKTO

(Plate II)

The picture of Hakto,[b] also a Zuñi katcina, shows a being with rounded helmet, having a characteristic Zuñi collar on its lower border. The face is painted green, with yellow and red marks on each temple. A horizontal bar, to the ends of which hang worsted and red horsehair, is attached to the top of the head.

Elk and deer horns are represented in both hands, and the kilt is made of buckskin.

CAIASTACANA

(Plate II)

This picture represents a Zuñi katcina of the same name,[c] which, like many others derived from this pueblo, has a collar on the lower rim of the helmet. On the right side of the head there is a horn, and on the left a projection the edges of which are terraced. A few yellow feathers appear in the hair. The artist has represented over a calico shirt a white cotton blanket with green and black border, the lower part of which partially conceals a ceremonial kilt.

In the left hand the figure carries a pouch of sacred meal, a crook,

---

[a] See Mrs Stevenson's article in Fifth Annual Report of the Bureau of American Ethnology, 1887, p. 533 et seq.

[b] This name is close to the Zuñian, and is probably derivative in Tusayan. For picture of doll see Internationales Archiv für Ethnographie, Band vii, pl. v, fig. 3.

[c] The meaning of the Zuñi name is "long horn."

PLATE II

PAUTIWA · CIPIKNE

HAKTO · CAIASTACANA

PLATE III

HUTUTU   HUIK

TCOLAWITZE   LOIICA

and a bow. It has a quiver full of arrows hung on the back, and a bundle of sheep scapulæ in the right hand. The leggings are fringed and the heel bands ornamented.

HUTUTU

(Plate III)

The figure of Hututu[a] differs from that of Caiastacana in wearing an antelope skin instead of a woman's white blanket. Its mask differs from that of the Zuñi being of the same name in having the terraced ornament on one side of the head replaced by a horn.

HUIK

(Plate III)

This katcina, which, like the preceding, appears in the Pamürti, has some of the facial symbols of the Snow katcina. There are two terraced rectangular designs on the face, one inclosing or surrounding each eye. Four large eagle feathers, two on each side, are attached longitudinally to the top of the head, and there are variegated feathers on the crown. The figure is bearded. The kilt is colored green, its lower margin being rimmed with a row of conical tinklers [b] resembling those on the kilts of the Snake priests.

TCOLAWITZE

(Plate III)

The Hopi artist gives a fair representation of Tcolawitze as he was personated, but has failed to draw the cedar-bark torch which he ordinarily carries.

He bears a bullroarer in the right hand, a bow and arrows in the left. He also has a few rats in one hand and a jack rabbit on his back, so that he is here depicted as he is often personated in rabbit hunts.[c]

In the Pamürti Tcolawitze was personated by a naked boy whose body was covered with round dots, painted with different colors, as shown in the picture.

LOIICA

(Plate III)

Traditions refer this personage to the Asa clan, which is commonly regarded of eastern origin. His picture is simple, with no characteristic symbolism.

---

[a] The name, which is the same in the Zuñi language, is probably derived from "Hu-tu-tu!" the peculiar cry of the personator.

[b] Deer hoofs, tin cones, or shells called mosilili, which occur in great numbers in ancient Arizona ruins, are ordinarily used for tinklers.

[c] The same personage with the same name occurs at Zuñi. See Journal of American Ethnology and Archæology, vol. I, 1891.

TCAKWAINA [a]

(Plate IV)

The matriarchal clan system is well preserved in the personages represented in the Tcakwaina katcina dances. In them there are the Tcakwaina men, the elder sister, the mother, the uncle, his brothers and sisters—in fact, representatives of the whole clan. The following pictures occur in the collection:

> Tcakwaina (male)
> Tcakwaina mana
> Tcakwaina yuadta (his mother)
> Tcakwaina taamû (their uncle)

These pictures afford interesting examples of katcinas introduced by a Tewan clan, the Asa, and when the personations or the drawings representing the Hopi personages are compared with those of Zuñi, eastern Keresan, and Tanoan pueblos, where similar Tcakwaina dances are celebrated, it will probably be found that there is a close resemblance between them. The Asa or Tcakwaina people also claim to have introduced into Tusayan Loiica and Kokopelli, pictures of which are given in plates III and XXV.

TCAKWAINA (MALE)

The picture of the male Tcakwaina has a black, glossy [b] face, with white bearded chin and serrated teeth. The yellow eyes are crescentic in form, and there is a warrior emblem attached to the hair. The shoulders are painted yellow, the body and upper arms black. As this being is regarded as a warrior, his picture shows a bow and arrows and a rattle. The kilt, probably buckskin, is undecorated, but is tied by a belt ornamented with the silver disks so common among Zuñis and Navahos.

A helmet of Tcakwaina which is said to be very ancient and to have been brought to Tusayan by the Asa people when they came from Zuñi is exhibited in one of the kivas at the festival of the winter solstice. The eyes of this mask are round instead of crescentic, and its snout is very protuberant. Curved sticks like those used by girls in dressing their hair are attached to this mask.

The introduction of a personation of Tcakwaina in the Pamürti is fitting, for this festival is the katcina return dance of the Tcakwaina or Asa clans. The Pamürti is a Zuñi dance, and the Asa are represented in Zuñi by descendants of those Asa women who remained there while the rest went on to Tusayan. This explains why the Zuñis claim this settlement as one of their pueblos in Tusayan.

---

[a] The name Tcakwaina is said to occur in Zuñian, Keresan, and Tanoan, as well as Hopi speech.

[b] Made so by use of albumen of egg. For picture of doll, see Internationales Archiv für Ethnographie, Band VII, pl. X, fig. 34.

PLATE IV

TCAKWAINA

TCAKWAINA TAAMU

TCAKWAINA MANA

TCAKWAINA YUADTA

PLATE V

SIO HUMIS

SIO HUMIS TAAMÛ

SIO AVATC HOYA

WÜWÜYOMO

Tcakwaina Mana

A number of traditions are extant regarding a warrior maiden who was dressing her hair in whorls above her ears when the pueblo in which she lived was attacked by hostiles. The men, according to these stories, were away when the attack began, and the defense fell upon the women. The girls, with their coiffures half made, seized bows and arrows and rushed to defend the pueblo. The eldest sisters of the Tcakwaina, often called the Tcakwaina maids, are mentioned in this connection, and the artist has pictorially represented this legend.

As shown, the hair on the right side of the head hangs loosely, tied in a bundle near the scalp, but on the left side it has been partly wound over the U-shaped stick[a] customarily used in making the headdress. To complete the coiffure this stick would have been drawn out, leaving the whorl, but, as the story goes, the enemy were upon them before this was possible, and the maids, with hair half dressed, seized the weapons of war, bows, and quivers of arrows, which the picture represents, and rushed to meet the foes.

The remainder of the symbolism on the face of the girl, as the picture shows, resembles that of her brother, save that the eyes are round and not crescentic. Like that of another maid called Hĕhĕĕ, who appears in the Powamû festival, this picture has a small beard below a hideous mouth.

Tcakwaina Yuadta

The picture of the mother of Tcakwaina (yuadta, his mother) has a general resemblance to that of her son and daughter (Tcakwaina mana), as here shown. She wears a black mask, and has a white mouth and red beard. Her eyes are lozenge shaped. Her black blanket is decorated with white crosses. She bears, as a warrior symbol, an eagle feather, stained red, tied to the crown of her head, and carries a rattle in her right hand.

Tcakwaina Taamû

The Tcakwaina uncle has little in common in symbolism with any ✓ of the other three; in fact, there is nothing which suggests the sister. The mask is painted green, with a border of red and yellow; the eyes are black, the beak is curved and pointed. The picture has a representation of a squash blossom on each side of the head and variegated feathers on the crown.

---

[a] As the mask exhibited in the Wikwaliobi kiva at Soyaluña has a crooked stick (gnela) attached to it, it may represent the ancient warrior maid, for a similar article is now used by Hopi girls in making their coiffures.

SEE HEARD MUS

SIO HUMIS

(Plate V)

The picture[a] representing a being called the Sio Humis or the Zuñi Humis has on the head a representation of a tablet with the upper border cut into three semicircles, symbols of rain clouds. The white figures painted on this tablet represent sprouting squash seeds, and the yellow disks sunflowers. The curved bands over the forehead are symbols of the rainbow. The face is divided by vertical bands into two fields of different colors, in which are representations of eyes and symbolic figures of sprouting gourds.

The figure has a rattle in the left hand and a sprig of pine in the right, and a turtle shell is tied to the right leg.

The supernatural here depicted was, according to legends, introduced from Zuñi during the present generation by a man now living in Hano, who has a large number of helmets bearing the above-described designs.

The meaning of the name Humis is doubtful. It is sometimes derived from Jemez, the name of an Eastern pueblo, and sometimes from humita, corn. The former derivation would appear more reasonable.

SIO HUMIS TAAMÛ [b]

(Plate V)

The picture gives a fair representation of the uncle of Sio Humis as personated in one of the dances of Pamürti. The rounded helmet has a single apical gourd horn, painted black and white at its junction with the helmet. On each side of the head is a symbolic squash blossom, made of a wooden cylinder with radiating sticks connected by yarn. A broad black band extends horizontally across the eyes, below which is an elongated snout. The neck has a collar of pine twigs, and to the back of the head are tied black and variegated feathers.

The figure has in its hands a yucca whip. The personator parades before the line of dancers with an ambling step, hooting as he goes.

SIO AVATC HOYA

(Plate V)

Men personating Sio Avatc hoya accompany those representing Sio Humis in the Pamürti. They are dressed as women and perform the same part as the katcina maids in some other dances; that is, they accompanied the songs with a rasping noise of sheep scapulæ scraped over a notched stick.

---

[a] For picture of the doll see Journal of American Ethnology and Archeology, vol. ii, 1892.
[b] Sio (Zuñi), Humis (Jemez or humita), taamû (their uncle).

In the pictures the masks are painted black, upon which field is a zigzag vertical median band with red borders. Their eyes are stellate, consisting of round spots from which radiate blue bands. The snout is prolonged, and attached to the left of the head there is an artificial squash-flower symbol, while on the right two eagle feathers, with a bundle of horsehair stained red, are tied vertically. Their kilts are decorated with triangular figures like those on women's blankets. They have sprigs of cedar in the belt and carry branches of the same tree in their hands.

WÜWÜYOMO

(Plate V)

The Honani clan at Sichumovi have in their keeping four disk-form masks, the symbolic markings of which resemble those of the sun mask of the Katcina clan. They were not worn in 1900, but in the festival of Pamürti were arranged, with four Zuñi Calako masks, on the floor in the house of the oldest woman of the Honani or Badger clan, in whose keeping they are, forming a kind of altar before which the men danced.

The artist has given a lateral view of a man wearing one of these objects.

The mask is flat and is divided by a median line into two parts, one green, the other yellow. The chin is painted black; the middle of the face is occupied by a black triangular design from which protrudes a snout curved upward. There are zigzag lines on the periphery of the mask, representing plaited corn husks, in which are inserted two kinds of feathers, three of which are longer than the remainder. There is a fox skin about the neck.

The blanket is white, undecorated, and covers a ceremonial kilt, the green border of which appears in the figure. The figure shows knit cotton leggings and heel bands decorated with stars or crosses. In the left hand is represented the skin meal pouch, and in the right a staff, both of which the personator is said to carry.

The symbolism of the mask as well as that of the dress is so close to that of Ahül that this being would seem to bear a relation to the Honani clan like that of Ahül to the Katcina clan.

Accompanying Wüwüyomo was a figure (not here reproduced) of his warrior companion, Kalektaka, who wears the warrior feathers on the head and a bandoleer over his shoulder, and carries a whizzer, a bow, and arrows. It was pointed out by several of the old Hopi priests that this particular warrior wears the embroidered parts of the sash in front of his waist, as the artist has represented it in his picture, instead of at one side, as is usually the case.

SIO CALAKO

(Plate VI)

This picture represents one of the Zuñi giants personated in Sichumovi in July,[a] whose masks were introduced from Zuñi by Saha, father of Supela, and are now in the keeping of the Honani clan, of which he was a member.

In the personation of these giants, the mask is fastened to a stick, which is carried aloft by a man concealed by blankets which are extended by hoops to form the body.

The head of the figure is surmounted by a crest of eagle feathers which are tipped with small breast feathers of the eagle. There are two lateral horns and a protruding snout; a symbol in the form of an arrowhead is painted on the forehead. The eyes are shown as globular, and are situated on a horizontal black band which crosses the upper part of the face, and around the neck is a collar of black feathers.

The body is represented as covered below with a blanket upon which are vertical masks representing feathers, or with a garment of feathers, characteristic of these giants, and over this, on the upper part of the body, is a representation of a white ceremonial blanket with triangular designs, symbols of rain clouds.

The helmets or masks of the Zuñi Calakos were displayed at Pamürti[b] with those of Wüwüyomo in the ancestral home of the Honani clan, to which they belong.

HELILÜLÜ

(Plate VI)

The figure of this katcina as drawn by the Hopi artist has two horizontal eagle feathers attached to the head and a cluster of red feathers and hair hanging on each side, which is a very uncommon feature.

The figure has a mountain lion skin around the neck, and is represented with yucca whips in the hands. The rows of small tin cone or shell rattles (called helilülü) along the lower rim of the kilt, shown in the picture, have probably led to the name by which it is known.

WOE

(Plate VI)

The symbolism of Woe katcina is a chevron across the nose, a symbolical design identical with that of the eagle, and figures of artificial flowers on the head. Two persons, a man and boy, represented the Woe katcina in a Buffalo dance in the winter of 1899–1900.

---

[a] For description of this dance, see Fifteenth Annual Report of the Bureau of American Ethnology, 1897, p. 30 et seq.

[b] This was highly appropriate, as this is a Zuñi dance and these masks were derived from Zuñi.

PLATE VI

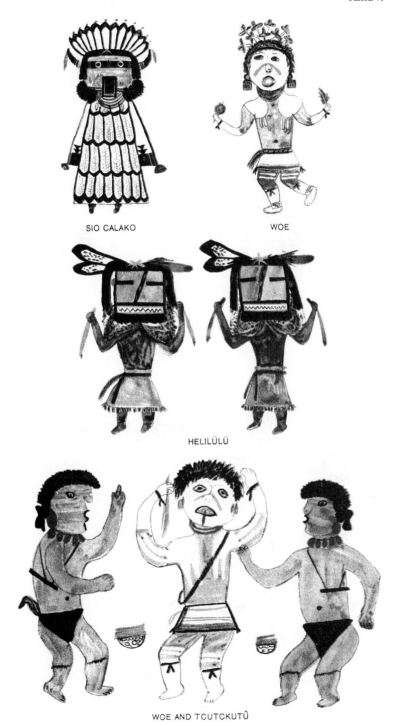

SIO CALAKO WOE

HELILÜLÜ

WOE AND TCUTCKUTÛ

PLATE VII

AHÜL

HAHAI WÜQTI

TUMAS

TUÑWUP

The eagle is symbolic of the sun or sky god, and its appearance in a Buffalo dance is appropriate, since the Buffalo girl wears a sun symbol on her back.

WOE AND TCUTCKUTÛ

(Plate VI)

Another picture represents Woe and two gluttons as they appear in one of the dances. The gluttons' bodies are painted yellow and their faces have red parallel bands across the cheeks extending from the eyes and the corners of the mouth to the ears.[a] They have ear pendants[b] and necklaces of rabbit's tails. Over the shoulder each has a bandoleer, to which a roll of paper-bread or piki is attached. Two bowls with bundles of food are drawn at the side of the main figure. Woe has a chevron design painted red on the nose and cheeks, turquoise ear pendants, and sheepskin wig. The legs, body, and arms are colored brown and white. The figure wears a bandoleer and white blanket, with red sash.

POWAMÛ FESTIVAL

The following personages appear in this festival:

Ahül.	Hehĕĕ.
Katcina mana and Kerwan.	Hehea.
Eototo and Woe.	Hehea mana.
Tumas and Tuñwup.	Telavai.
Hahai wüqti and Natacka mana.	Powamû.
Tehabi and Tuñwup taamû.	Wüwüyomo.
Natacka naamû.	Atocle.
Kumbi Natacka.	Awatobi Soyok taka.
Soyok wüqti.	Awatobi Soyok wüqti.

AHÜL

(Plate VII)

The figure of Ahül has all the symbolism characteristic of this god when personated as leader of the katcinas in their annual return to Walpi in the Powamû festival.

The disk-shaped mask is crossed by horizontal bands painted white and black, separating the face into a lower part, colored black, and an upper, which is divided into yellow and green zones, the former being turned to the observer. Black crosses cover these two upper zones. In the middle of the face is painted a triangular black figure, and to the middle of the horizontal bands which separate the chin from the two upper zones there is attached a curved representation of the beak, painted green.

The zigzag lines around the periphery of the disk represent plaited corn husks in which are inserted eagle or turkey feathers, the tips of

---

a The same markings that the Tataukyamû priests bear in the New-fire ceremony.

b These decorations adorn the Tataukyamû priests.

which are colored black. The red lines interspersed with these feathers represent horsehair stained red.

The reddish-brown body about the neck represents a fox skin, the legs and bushy tail of which are indicated.

The picture shows a ceremonial blanket or kilt, colored green, with embroidered edge, around the body, and a similar kilt on the loins. The ceremonial dance sash is represented on one side, hanging down to the right knee.

The network leg-covering represents the garment worn by the sun god, and the row of globular bodies down each leg are shell tinklers. The moccasins are painted green and the anklets are ornamented with terrace designs in red, representing rain clouds.

In the left hand there are a small meal pouch made of a fox skin with dependent tail, a bundle of bean sprouts painted green, and a slat of wood, dentate at each end, representing a chief's badge. In the right hand is a staff, on the top of which are drawn two eagle feathers and a few red horsehairs. Midway in its length is tied an ear of corn, a crook, and attached breast feathers of the eagle.

HAHAI WÜQTI

(Plate VII)

The picture of Hahai wüqti, like that of Kokyan (spider) wüqti (woman), has eyes of crescentic form. The hair is done up in two elongated bodies which hang by the sides of her head, and she has a bang of red horsehair on the forehead. She wears a red fox skin around her neck, and to her waist are tied two sashes, the extremities of which, highly embroidered, are shown in the picture. In her right hand she carries a gourd.[a]

Hahai wüqti appears in the kiva exhibition of Palülükoñti, or Añkwañti, when she offers sacred meal to the Snake effigies for food and presents her breasts to them to suckle. The best representation of Hahai wüqti is at Powamû, when she accompanies her children, the monsters called Natackas. In both festivals she wears the paraphernalia shown in the figure.[b]

TUMAS

(Plate VII)

Tumas is the mother of Tuñwup, who flogs the children in the Powamû festival. Her mask, as shown in the drawing,[c] has fan-like

---

[a] The mask of the Soyal katcina, Ahülani, has similar marks in alternate celebrations of the Soyaluña. Pictures of the sun have been drawn for the author with similar crescentic eyes, from which it is inferred that Ahülani is a sun god who appears as a bird (eagle) man in Soyaluña and that Hahai wüqti and Kokyan wüqti are different names of the same supernatural.

[b] For photograph of Hahai wüqti, Natacka naamû, and Soyok mana, see Fifteenth Annual Report Bureau of American Ethnology, 1897, pl. CVI. For picture of doll, see Internationales Archiv für Ethnographie, Band VII, pl. IX, fig. 27.

[c] For picture of doll, see Internationales Archiv für Ethnogrpaphie, Band VII, pl. XI, fig. 41. Both Tumas and Tuñwup have several aliases in different Hopi pueblos; at Oraibi the latter is known as Ho katcina.

appendages made of crow feathers on each side. On the top of the head are parrot feathers and breast feathers of the eagle. The edge of the mask is surrounded by woven yarn colored black and red. The face, which is painted blue, is almost covered by a triangular black figure rimmed with white occupying the position of the mouth.

A fox skin is about her neck; she wears a woman's decorated blanket, and carries a meal plaque in her hands. When the flogging of children takes place at Hano, Tumas stands at the foot of the kiva ladder while her two sons, called Tuñwup, perform this act.

TUÑWUP

(Plate VII)

With the picture of Tumas the Hopi artist has also introduced figures of her two sons, Tuñwup, as they appear in the child-flogging in Powamû. Tuñwup has a white mask with black, prominent eyes. An arrow-shaped figure is painted on the forehead, and there is a horn on each side of the head.[a]

The mouth is large, of rectangular shape, and there is a fox skin about the neck. The body is painted black with parallel vertical white markings. A belt made of ears of different-colored corn strung together girts the waist. The kilt is made of a fringe of red horsehair, and the heel bands are of the same material. There is a yucca whip in each hand.

Details of the ceremonial Powamû child flogging at Walpi and Hano vary somewhat. In the Hano celebration an altar is made in the kiva at that time by the chiefs, Anote and Satele, both of whom place their official badges upon a rectangle of meal drawn on the kiva floor. Into this rectangle the children are led by their foster parents and flogged in the presence of the inhabitants of the pueblo.

The two floggers, Tuñwup, stand one on each side of the figure made of meal, holding their whips of yucca. As they dance they strike the boys or girls before them as hard as they can, after which they pass the whips to a priest standing by. After each flogging the yucca whips are waved in the air, which is called the purification. After the children have been flogged many adults, both men and women, present their bared bodies, legs, and arms to the blows of the yucca whips.

In a dance in the Walpi kivas, at the opening of the Powamû festival, in which fifteen or twenty Tuñwups were personated, several of their number, as well as spectators, were terribly flogged on bare backs and abdomens.

As the figure of Tuñwup is a conspicuous one on the altar of the

---

[a] The symbolism of Tuñwup resembles that of Calako, whom the author identifies as a sun god. Traditions declare that the first youths were flogged by Calako.

Niman Katcina in several Hopi pueblos, it is probable that this super-natural being was introduced from a ruin called Kicuba, once inhabited by the Katcina clan.

The following beings form the Tuñwup group, personations of the ancients of the Katcina clan:

> Tuñwup tatakti (men).
> Tumas (mother of Tuñwup).
> Tuñwup taamû (their uncle).

TEHABI AND TUÑWUP TAAMÛ

(Plate VIII)

A drawing of a mudhead clown bearing on his back a figure resembling Tuñwup was identified as representing Tehabi. These two were accompanied by a third figure called Tuñwup taamû (Tuñwup, their uncle), the whole picture representing an episode in one of the ceremonies.

Tuñwup's uncle has a green mask, two horns, great goggle-eyes, and a black band with upright parallel white lines across the face. The figure is bearded and has a fox skin about the neck. The body is daubed black, but wears a white ceremonial kilt with red and black border, which is tied to the waist by a large white cotton kilt. Like his nephew, he carries yucca whips.

KERWAN AND KATCINA MANA

(Plate VIII)

These two figures illustrate one of the most beautiful incidents in Powamû, when the beans which have been artificially sprouted in the kivas are brought out into the plazas and distributed. The two figures represent male and female persons, and between them is a flat basket in which are carried the bean sprouts which have been grown in the kiva.

Kerwan has a green mask with eyes and mouth indicated by black crescents. On the top of the head there are two eagle tail feathers and a cluster of parrot and eagle breast feathers. The female figure has hair hanging down the back, a yellow masquette with red horse-hair before the face, and an eagle breast feather on the crown of the head. She wears a woman's blanket tied about the waist with a large cotton belt, the whole covered by a white blanket.

SOYOKOS (MONSTERS)

The name Soyoko is applied to certain monsters called Natackas, which appear in Powamû. There are three sets of Natacka masks on the East mesa—one in Hano, in the keeping of the Tobacco clan, now hanging in a back room of Anote's house; another in Sichumovi; and a third set in Walpi.

PLATE VIII

TEHABI   TUÑWUP TAAMÛ

KERWAN AND MANA

PLATE IX

KUTCA NATACKA

KUMBI NATACKA

NATACKA NAAMÛ

These Natackas are undoubtedly derived from eastern pueblos, for they are represented at Zuñi by the so-called Natackó, which they closely resemble in symbolism. They were introduced into Tusayan by the Tanoan colonists, the Asa and the Hano clans, the Middle mesa Natackas being simply derived from the East mesa. They are not found at Oraibi, as these clans are not represented there.

Besides the Soyoko or monsters which regularly appear in the Walpi Powamû, there are other similar bogies which make occasional visits. Two of these, called Awatobi Soyok taka and Soyok wüqti, were derived from Awatobi, one, Atocle, from Zuñi, and one, Tcabaiyo,[a] is of unknown derivation. All apparently have the same function, but there is only a remote similarity in their symbolism.

The name Soyok or Soyukû, given by the Hopi to the Natackas, is linguistically a Keresan word, and as the mythologic conceptions and objective symbolism are very similar in the two stocks, we may regard the Hopi being as a derivation from the Keresan. The fact that these personages are found in the Hopi pueblos where there are other evidences of incorporation from eastern pueblos tells in favor of the theory that they were brought to Tusayan from eastern pueblos.

In the personation of Natacka we find also a person called naamû, their father. The following list includes the varieties of these personations:

Nanatacka tatakti (males).
Nanatacka civaamû (their sisters).
Natacka wüqti (mother).
Natacka naamû (their father).

NATACKA NAAMÛ

(Plate IX)

The father as figured by the artist has on the head a crest of turkey tail feathers and two eagle feathers, each tipped with a red breast feather. He has a goggle-eyed black mask with a trifid symbol on the forehead and a curved horn on each side of the head.

The father of the Natackas appears at Powamû with their sisters and Hahai wüqti, and the three visit all the houses of the pueblos.[b]

During these visits Hahai wüqti carries on a conversation with inmates of the houses in a falsetto voice, and gives to the men or boys a mouse trap made of yucca fiber, and a stick, telling them that in eight days she will return with her children, the Natackas; that they must trap game and procure meat for these when they come. To the woman of the house Hahai wüqti gives an ear of corn, telling her to grind it and have meal and bread for the Natackas when they return.

---

a The mask is owned by the Snake clan. Atocle at Zuñi is sometimes called Soyok.

b There are three groups, one for each pueblo on the East mesa.

KUMBI NATACKA

(Plate IX)

The black Natacka has a black mask with goggle eyes and with a green arrowhead on the forehead. It has two horns, one of which the artist has represented, and a crest of conventional eagle wing feathers rising from a bunch of black feathers on the back of the head. A fox skin hangs about the neck. Kumbi Natacka wears a buckskin garment over a calico shirt, and carries a saw in one hand, a hatchet in the other. The black objects hanging over the shoulder are locks of hair, from which depend eagle tail feathers.

The small figure accompanying Kumbi Natacka represents a Hehea katcina, two or more of which go with the Natackas in their begging trip through the pueblos. The body is covered with phallic symbols, and a lasso is carried in the right hand. The leggings are of sheepskin stained black. The face has the characteristic zigzag symbols of Hehea.[a]

KUTCA NATACKA

(Plate IX)

The white Natacka resembles the black, save that the mask is white instead of black. He also carries a saw in his right hand, and a yucca whip in his left. In the personations of this Natacka the men, as a rule, carry bows and arrows in their left hands.

There are also Natackas of other colors which the artist has not figured.

NATACKA WÜQTI, OR SOYOK WÜQTI

(Plate X)

Soyok wüqti[b] has a large black mask with great yellow goggle eyes, and red beard and hair, in which is tied a red feather, symbol of death or war. She carries in one hand a crook to which several shell rattles (mosilili) are attached, and in the other a huge knife. She is much feared by the little children, who shudder as she passes through the pueblos and halts to threaten with death those she meets. She appears at Powamû at about the same time as the Natackas, but does not accompany them.

The episode illustrated by the figure shows an interview of the Soyok woman and a lad who is crying with fright. The woman has demanded food of the boy, and he offers a rat on the end of a stick. The bogy shakes her head, demanding a jack rabbit which the boy carries in his right hand.

---

[a] For figure of the doll see Internationales Archiv für Ethnographie, Band VII, pl. IX, fig. 30.
[b] Soyok from skoyo, a Keresan word meaning monster or bogy.

PLATE X

NATACKA WÜQTI, OR SOYOK WÜQTI

PLATE XI

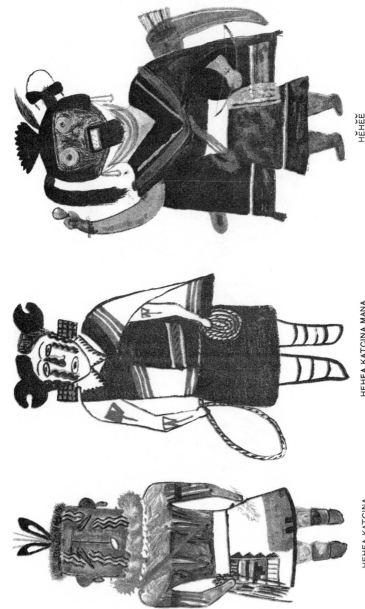

HĔHĔĔ

HEHEA KATCINA MANA

HEHEA KATCINA

NATACKA MANA

The sister of the Natackas, called also Natacka mana and Soyok mana,[a] accompanies her brothers on their begging trip through the pueblos of the East mesa. Her picture represents a person with black mask and white chin, and with hair arranged in two whorls over the ears, as is customary with maidens. She has round, green eyes, a square mouth with red teeth, and a beard. On her back she carries a basket suspended by a band which passes across her forehead. In this basket she collects the meat and bread which the Natackas obtain from the different households. Her clothing is a woman's blanket, over which is thrown a buckskin, and she carries in one hand a large knife.

HEHEA

(Plate XI)

Hehea katcina, like many others, may be personated without kilt or in complete dress. In the former case a sheepskin replacing an old-time buffalo skin is hung over the shoulder and phallic emblems are painted on arms, legs, and body. The mask is decorated with the zigzag marking on each cheek. In this form Hehea appears in certain kiva exercises at the ceremonial grinding of meal by the Aña katcina manas. We also find him associated with the Corn maids and with the Natackas. The phallic symbols are depicted on the bodies of the Wüwütcimtû and Tataukyamû in the New-fire ceremony, and there are other evidences which associate the former with Hehea.

A picture of this form of Hehea was drawn, but has not been reproduced. It represents a large and small Hehea, each with characteristic zigzag symbols on the face and with oblique eyes and mouth. Both have phallic symbols on body and limbs, and wear artificial flowers on their heads.[b]

The body has a sheepskin covering stained black and leggings of same material, which have replaced buffalo skins formerly used for the same purpose. Each carries a lariat, the use of which is explained in the account of the visits of the Natackas on their begging trips to different houses.

Another picture of Hehea, which also represents a primitive conception of this personage, has a kilt and the elaborate dress in which he sometimes appears in ceremonial public dances. It is reproduced in plate XI.

[a] This part is taken by a lad. For picture of the doll see Internationales Archiv für Ethnographie, Band VII, pl. IX.

[b] Compare this artificial flower with that of the Wüwütcimtû society. The members of both this society and the Tataukyamû have similar phallic symbols painted on body and limbs. For a picture of the doll, see Internationales Archiv für Ethnographie, Band VII, pls. VII, VIII, figs. 16, 18.

Hehea is evidently an ancient katcina,[a] and from his appearance in many primitive ceremonies, public and secret, we may regard him as connected with a very old ritual.

The Wüwütcimtû priests in the New-fire celebration at Walpi often decorate their faces (masks are not used in this rite) with the symbols of Hehea, and he is intimately associated with Corn maids (Palahiko mana)[b] of the Mamzrau festival.

HEHEA MANA

(Plate XI)

The Hehea mana, sister of Hehea, accompanies the Natacka group in Powamû. She is represented by the artist with the characteristic coiffure of a maiden, and has the same zigzag facial lines as her brother. On her arms are the same phallic symbols, and in her hand she carries a lariat.

If any one refuses to grant the requests of the Natackas for meat or food, both she and her brother try to lasso the delinquent.

HÉHÉÉ

(Plate XI)

This figure represents a warrior maid who sometimes appears in Powamû. There is such a close resemblance between her and Tcakwaina mana (see page 63) that they would seem to be identical personages. The reason for her unfinished coiffure is given in the account of the Tcakwaina maid.

AWATOBI SOYOK TAKA

(Plate XII)

The massacre at Awatobi took place just two centuries ago, but there are several katcinas surviving in Walpi which are said to have been derived from that pueblo. Among these may be mentioned two bogies called Soyok taka and Soyok mana, male and female monsters. These are occasionally personated at Walpi, and, as their names imply, originally came from Awatobi. Soyok taka corresponds with Natacka, and probably both originally came to Tusayan from eastern pueblos.

Soyok taka wears a mask without distinct symbolism, and has a protuberant snout, with teeth made of corn husks. He has goggle eyes and hair hanging down over his face. His garment is a rabbit-skin rug, and, like Natacka, he carries a saw.[c] On his back hangs a basket containing a child whom he has captured.

---

[a] Perhaps derived from Awatobi.

[b] The Corn maids have several different names, varying with clans. For picture of doll in which this association appears, see Internationales Archiv für Ethnographie, Band VII, pl. x, fig. 31.

[c] A modern innovation in both instances.

PLATE XII

AWATOBI SOYOK TAKA

AWATOBI SOYOK WÜQTI

PLATE XIII

TCABAIYO

ATOCLE

AWATOBI SOYOK WÜQTI

(Plate XII)

The figure of the Awatobi Soyok woman differs but little from that of the Walpi, but has prominent corn-husk teeth and two white parallel bars on each cheek. These two symbols were in fact said to distinguish the Awatobi from the Walpi Soyok wüqti; several priests called attention to the differences when the pictures were shown them.

TCABAIYO

(Plate XIII)

Tcabaiyo is still another of the bogy gods. The mask belongs to Hoñyi, of the Snake clan, who always personates this being. The picture represents him in the act of seizing a small boy who, from the zigzag marks on his face and the sheepskin blanket, may be a Hehea child.

Tcabaiyo is threatening to kill the boy with the great knife which he carries in his left hand. In the picture the black mask has a long swollen proboscis. The eyes are protuberant, and there is a broad-headed arrow in the middle of the forehead. A white crescent is painted on the cheek. Feathers of the eagle wing form a fan-shaped crest, and a bunch of feathers is tied to the back of the helmet. Tcabaiyo wears a fox skin about the neck. Feathers of the eagle tail are attached to his upper arm. The red-colored garment represents a buckskin; that part of the dress in the form of a white man's waistcoat is an innovation. Arms and legs are spotted with black dots and the breech clout is held in place by an embroidered sash.

Tcabaiyo occasionally appears in Powamû and his symbolism has a close likeness to that of other Natackas or Soyokos. Though he is referred to the Soyoko or Natacka group, he is supposed to be derived from a different clan, and he bears a name characteristic of that clan.

ATOCLE

(Plate XIII)

There is still another of these Soyokos (monsters) whose functions are nearly the same as those of the sister or mother of the Natackas. This personage has a Zuñi name, Atocle,[a] which betrays her origin. Atocle is an old woman, personated by a man, who goes about the Zuñi pueblo frightening children in much the same way that Soyok wüqti does at Walpi.

---

[a] The actions of this person at Zuñi are described in the Journal of American Ethnology and Archeology, vol. II, 1892, where she is called an old scold.

The Hopi variant, as shown in the picture, has a black helmet with projecting flat snout, and a mass of hair to which is attached a red feather. In one hand is a bow and arrows, in the other a knife, suggesting weapons for her function. She is accompanied by a clown, who holds her back by a lasso tied about her waist.

SO WŬQTI

(Plate XIV)

So wŭqti, Grandmother woman, is here represented by the Hopi artist as clasping hands with her child, a Powamû katcina. On each cheek there is a red spot, and in her hair is an artificial flower. She carries on her back Hehea, her grandchild, as the zigzag marks on his face clearly indicate, and has a pine bough in her hand. The fact that her grandchild has Hehea symbols would seem to refer her to the group to which the latter and his sister belong.

MASAUÛ

(Plate XIV)

The picture of Masauû has a round helmet decorated with spots of different colors. At the top of this helmet there are many twigs, to which prayer feathers (nakwakwocis) are attached. There is a decorated kilt around the neck, and a rabbit-skin rug, shirt, and kilt about the body. The legs and arms are painted red and spotted black. The two rings on the breast are parts of a necklace made of human bones. The figure carries a yucca whip in each hand.

EOTOTO

(Plate XIV)

This is one of the most important katcinas, and is very prominent in several celebrations.

The artist's picture of Eototo has a white head covering, with small holes for eyes and mouth, and diminutive ear appendages. There is a fox skin about the neck.

The blanket is white, and is worn over a white kilt tied with an embroidered sash, the ends of which are seen below. The figure also has knit hose and heel bands. In the left hand there is a skin pouch of sacred meal and a chief's badge [a] (moñkohû), while the right hand carries a bundle of sheep scapulæ and a gourd bottle with water from a sacred spring.[b]

Eototo is one of the most prominent masked personages at Walpi

---

[a] See Journal of American Ethnology and Archæology, vol. II, 1892. For picture of doll, see Internationales Archiv für Ethnographie, Band VII, pl. IX, fig. 24.

[b] The use of this water and sacred meal is described in the Journal of American Ethnology and Archæology, vol. II, 1892.

PLATE XIV

POWAMÛ

SO WÜQTI

MASAUÛ

EOTOTO

PLATE XV

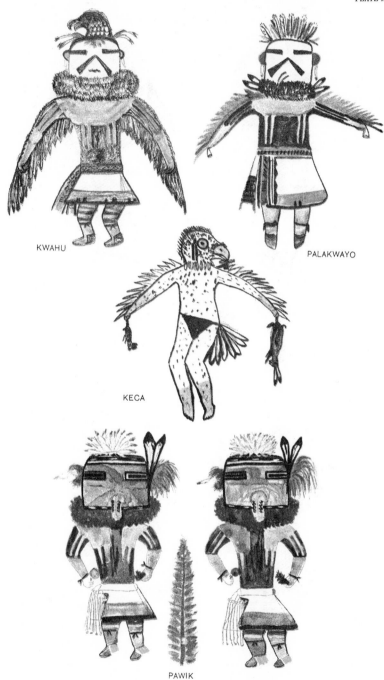

KWAHU

PALAKWAYO

KECA

PAWIK

in the celebration of the Departure of the Katcinas. On the last morning of that festival he is accompanied by three other katcinas who march around the kiva entrance, holding conversation with the chief below and receiving offerings, as has been described elsewhere.[a]

The god Eototo was introduced from the old pueblo, Sikyatki, and his old mask or helmet is in the keeping of the descendants of the Kokop family, which once inhabited that pueblo. The close similarity in symbolic designs to Masauû, also a Sikyatki god, shows that the two names are virtually dual appellations of the same mythological conception, but that they originated in this pueblo is not yet proved.

One of the most interesting personations of Masauû appeared in Powamû in 1900, when a man represented this god in the five Walpi kivas. He wore a helmet made of a large gourd, pierced with openings for eyes and mouth and painted black with micaceous hematite sprinkled over them. He and a companion carried old-fashioned planting sticks and imitated planting, while about twenty unmasked men, representing a chorus called Maswik[b] katcinas, some personating males, others females, danced and sang about them.

At the close of the personation in each kiva, the representative of Masauû was loaded with prayer offerings. This archaic ceremony was regarded with great reverence and was shunned by all save the initiated.

KWAHU

(Plate XV)

Kwahu, the Eagle katcina, is figured in the drawing with an eagle's head above the helmet in a way that recalls an Aztec picture. The characteristic symbolic marks of certain birds of prey, as the eagle and hawk, are the chevron marks on the face, which are well shown in this picture.

In personations of this and other birds the wings are represented by a string of feathers tied to the arms, as shown in the picture.

PALAKWAYO

(Plate XV)

The symbolism of Palakwayo, the Red Hawk, is similar to that of Türpockwa, but there is no bird's head above the helmet. The figure also has the moisture tablet on the back. In each of the outstretched hands is carried a bell.

---

[a] See Journal of American Ethnology and Archæology, vol. ii, 1892.
[b] Masauû, wik (bearers).

KECA

(Plate XV)

The figure of Keca, the Kite, has two parallel black marks on each side of the face, not unlike the facial symbols of the war god, Püükoñ hoya. The body is white with black spots representing feathers, but the forearms and legs are painted yellow. The wings are imitated by a row of feathers tied to the arms, and the tail by feathers attached to the breechclout. Keca holds in his left hand a hare and in his right a rabbit.

PAWIK [a]

(Plate XV)

Pawik, the Duck katcina, is represented in the accompanying pictures. The helmet is green with a long curved snout painted yellow, around the base of which is tied wool stained red. The eyes are rectangular, the left yellow, the right blue. Two upright eagle feathers are attached to the left side of the helmet, near which is a bunch of horsehair stained red. On the right side of the helmet is tied an ovoid symbol of an undeveloped squash with a breast feather of the eagle projecting from one pole and red horsehair about its base of attachment. The upper part of the helmet is girt by parallel bands of black, yellow, and red. The lower rim has a black band in which there are patches of white. The tree represented between the two figures is the pine.

TOTCA

(Plate XVI)

Totca, the Humming Bird, has a globular head painted blue, with long pointed beak. The dorsal part of the body is colored green, the ventral yellow. The rows of feathers down the arms are wings, by a movement of which the flight of a bird is imitated.

MONWÛ AND KOYIMSI

(Plate XVI)

This personation of the Owl has a helmet with rows of parellel yellow, green, red, and black crescents, and a prominent hooked beak. He wears a rabbit-skin blanket tied by an embroidered sash, and holds a bow and arrows in one hand and a rattle in the other. The figure is accompanied by a clown who has a feather in each hand.

---

[a] For description of Pawik katcina see Tusayan Katcinas, Fifteenth Annual Report of the Bureau of Ethnology, 1897, pages 299–303.

PLATE XVI

TOTCA

MONWÛ

KOYIMSI

MONWÛ WÜQTI

PLATE XVII

SALAB MONWÛ

HOTSKO

TÜRPOCKWA

YAUPA

MONWÛ WÜQTI

(Plate XVI)

The Owl woman and her two young are figured in this picture, and need no explanation additional to that given of the Owl katcina with whom she is associated.

SALAB MONWÛ

(Plate XVII)

The head shown in this picture is readily recognized as that of an Owl. He wears a kilt made of buckskin, and has a belt with silver disks. He carries a pine branch and bow in the left hand, a rattle in the right.

HOTSKO

(Plate XVII)

The figure of Hotsko is owl-like, with broad mouth, and wears a rabbit-skin rug tied on the body by an embroidered sash. This picture evidently represents a bird, but the author can not identify it.

TÜRPOCKWA

(Plate XVII)

The picture of this bird has a helmet surmounted by a bird's head, like that of the eagle, and a black chevron on the face. The beak is long and slender.

Türpockwa, like many other birds, has a moisture or sun tablet on the back, the horizontal plumes of which show on each side of the neck. The personator's arms, here extended, have attached feathers like wings. The dress and other paraphernalia shown in the figure can hardly be regarded as characteristic.

YAUPA

(Plate XVII)

Yaupa, the Mocking Bird, has a helmet painted white, with a triangular design on the face, to the sides of which ring-like figures are attached. The beak is long and slender, and there are clusters of bright parrot feathers on the top of the head; indications of the wings are shown in the black lines along the arms. The spots on the body represent feathers.

HOSPOA

(Plate XVIII)

Hospoa, the Road Runner, as shown in the picture, has a green helmet covered with rows of black and white crescents, a short beak, and stellate eyes.

On the back this bird has a painted skin stretched over a framework, called a moisture tablet. To each upper corner are attached two feathers, which project horizontally, and along the edges is a string with attached horsehair stained red.

There is a flute in one hand, a rattle in the other. The garments are a ceremonial kilt, girdle, and embroidered sash.

PATSZRO

(Plate XVIII)

Patszro, the Snipe katcina, has a figure of the snipe painted on the forehead, a long, slender beak, and semicircular markings on each cheek. These markings consist of white, red, and yellow bands, the first furnished with a row of black wings.

The body is naked, painted white on the ventral, green on the dorsal side. The tail feathers are tied to the belt in such a way that their extremities show behind.

The spots on the body represent small downy feathers attached by means of gum or some sticky substance.

KOYONA

(Plate XVIII)

Koyona, the Turkey, has a green-colored helmet, with long extended beak and bright red wattles, which are made of flannel cloth. The wings and tail are made of feathers attached to the arms and belt. There are many small feathers attached to the body with gum.

KOWAKO

(Plate XVIII)

The picture of Kowako, the Chicken katcina, has a red comb and wattles; the body is painted red on the dorsal, white on the ventral side.

The personator wears a ceremonial white kilt with embroidered green border worked into rain-cloud symbols. The wattles and comb are made of red flannel, and feathers are tied to the arms for wings.

The figures of both Koyona and Kowako (Chicken) which the Hopis made are more realistic than the personations which were seen by the author, although the latter wear elaborate masks, with wattles, comb,

PLATE XVIII

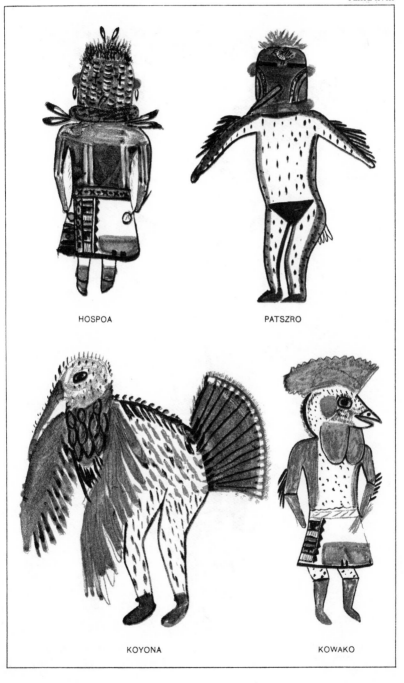

HOSPOA

PATSZRO

KOYONA

KOWAKO

PLATE XIX

MOMO

TETAÑAYA

and beak, which are fine imitations of the heads of these birds. The realism of these masks, as compared with the conventionalism of the masks of Patszro, Kwayo, and others, would indicate the later introduction of Koyona and Kowako into the katcina cult.

MOMO

(Plate XIX)

Momo, the Bee katcina, has a yellow head with black crescentic bands extending on each side from the globular eyes. The back of the head is banded yellow and green, and on the crown there are pedunculated bodies arranged in a row, with two long, stiff, black projections representing antennæ. There are also feathers on the back of the helmet. He carries a miniature bow and arrows. In the dance he imitates the hum of a bee, and goes from one spectator to another, shooting the blunt arrows at them. To still the cries of children, due to mere fright, the Bee katcina squirts a little water on the supposed wound.[a]

TETAÑAYA

(Plate XIX)

The picture of the Wasp katcina has body, legs, arms, and mask painted with parallel lines of green, brown, red, yellow, and black. There are two straight vertical horns on the head and a long slim proboscis, also banded with black and white. This being is only occasionally personated in the winter ceremonies.

TELAVAI

(Plate XX)

On the morning of the last day of Powamû, the beans which have sprouted in the kivas are plucked up and distributed by masked persons to all the people in the pueblos, who boil and eat them as a great relish. Each of the nine kivas delegates two or more men to distribute the sprouts grown in that kiva. From the fact that these men distribute the bean sprouts at early dawn, they are called Telavai (Dawn), although they represent Malo, Owa, Tacab, or others.

There are in the collection a number of paintings to which this name was given which did not appear in the Powamû in 1900.

The distinctive symbolism of Telavai is a rain-cloud design on each cheek, and eyes that are each represented by a band having one end curved. There are four horizontally arranged eagle feathers on top of the helmet, surmounted by a cluster of variegated feathers.

---

[a] In 1900 a small syringe was used for this purpose.

OWA

(Plates XX, LXIII)

The figure of Owa has a helmet mask colored green, with yellow, red, and black lines drawn diagonally across the cheeks. The snout is protuberant and the eyes are represented by black bands. The hair hangs down the back. Parrot and eagle feathers are attached to the crown of the head.

The body is painted red, and there are parallel yellow bands on body, arms, and legs. The ceremonial kilt about the loins is tied by a woman's belt and embroidered sack. A fox skin sometimes depends from the rear. Under the right knee is represented a turtle-shell rattle, and the figure has moccasins and heel bands.

Owa carries a bow and arrows in the left hand, and a small gourd rattle in the right. These are the presents which this being commonly makes to children in the Powamû festival.

MALO

(Plate XXI)

In a drawing of Malo katcina the artist has represented the main symbols of this being as he is seen when personated in dances.

The face is crossed by an oblique medial band, in which are rows of spots. The face on one side of this band is painted yellow, on the other green. The figure has a representation of a squash blossom on the right side of the head and two eagle feathers on the left, to which is attached a bundle of horsehair stained red.[a]

HUMIS

(Plate XXI)

The figure of Humis katcina shows a helmet with a terraced tablet, symbolic of rain clouds. To the highest point are attached two eagle feathers, and to each of the angles of the lateral terrace a turkey tail feather and a sprig of grass. The whole tablet is rimmed with red and painted green, with designs upon it. Symbols of sprouting corn and terraced rain clouds appear on the flat sides.

The face of the helmet is divided medially by a black band, in which are three white rings. On the right half of the face, which is blue, there is on each side of the eye-slit a symbol of the sprouting squash or gourd, replaced on the left side of the face by small symbols of rain clouds. Humis has a collar of pine boughs, sprigs of which are also inserted in the armlets, the belt and the kilt. The body is smeared with corn smut, and there are two pairs of crescents, painted black,

---

[a] For description of Malo katcina, see Journal of American Ethnology and Archæology, vol. II, 1892. For picture of the doll, see Internationales Archiv für Ethnographie, Band VII, pl. VIII, fig. 21.

PLATE XX

TELAVAI

OWA AND MANA

PLATE XXI

MALO

HUMIS

HOPI AVATC HOYA

HUHUAN

on the abdomen. Humis carries a rattle in the right hand and a sprig of pine in the left. A small black stick is tied to his left wrist.

The two figures which accompany Humis represent Hano clowns, who are accustomed to amuse the audience during the celebration of the dances in which he appears.

Each clown wears a cap with two straight horns made of leather, with corn husks tied to the tops. The horns are banded alternately black and white, as are also the body, arms, and legs. The figure to the left has a bowl filled with Hopi wafer bread before him: the one at the right carries a roll of the same in his right hand.

The name Humis is supposed to have been derived from the pueblo Jemez in New Mexico and to be the same as the Zuñi Hemacikwi, a dance which is ordinarily celebrated in summer.

HOPI AVATC HOYA

(Plate XXI)

The Hopi Avatc hoya accompanies the Humis katcina, and, as may be seen by consulting the pictures, differs widely from the Sio (Zuñi) Avatc hoya. The mask is painted black, with white rings; the body, arms, and legs, are painted red, with white rings on the body and arms, and with black rings on the legs. The mouth and eyes are represented by green rings. He wears cones made of corn husks in his ears and curved feathers on the head.[a]

HUHUAN

(Plate XXI)

The pictures of Huhuan represent beings with a characteristic gait, who appear in Powamû, when they distribute gifts from one of the kivas.

They wear sheepskin caps and necklaces of mosaic ear pendants. They should not be confounded with the Barter katcinas, who trade dolls, etc., in certain festivals. Their symbolic markings are a checker band of white and colored squares covering the helmet.

NÜVAK

(Plate XXII)

There are three pictures of Nüvak, the Snow katcina, two of which represent male personages and one a female. The latter is called the Cold-bringing woman, and is possibly mother of the former.

This personage[b] is regarded by all the Hopi as a Hano (Tanoan) katcina, and the dance in which he figures is said to have been derived from the far east.

---

[a] For picture of doll, see Internationales Archiv für Ethnographie, Band VII, pl. IX, fig. 29.

[b] For picture of doll, see same volume, pl. V, fig. 4.

Near the settlement of Hano people at Isba, Coyote spring, not far from the Government House, but on the right of the road from Keams Canyon, there is a large spring called Moñwiva, which is sacred to the Plumed Snake of Hano. In the March festival, effigies of this monster are carried to this spring, where certain ceremonies are performed similar to those which the Walpians observe[a] at Tawapa.

A year ago (1899) this spring, which had become partially filled with sand, was dug out and walled, at which time an elaborate masked dance representing Nüvak katcina was performed near it. This intimate association between Palülükoñ (Plumed Snake) and Nüvak (Snow) appears on a mask of the latter, presently described and figured.

The picture of one form of Snow katcina, shown in the accompanying figure, has rectangular terraced designs on the back of the head and zigzag sticks representing lightning snakes on the upper edge. The figure wears a white blanket reversed. The picture shows the stitches of the embroidery on the lower margin.

A second figure of the Snow katcina, on which the predominant color is green instead of white, is readily distinguished from the former by figures of snakes' heads painted on each cheek. It has the same four lightning symbols on the head and two eagle tail feathers. This figure wears an ordinary dance kilt, embroidered with rain-cloud and falling-rain designs, and held in place by a girdle. It carries a flute in one hand.

YOHOZRO WÜQTI [b]

(Plate XXII)

The Cold-bringing woman, who is connected with the Nüvak or Snow katcina, is claimed by the people of Hano as one of their supernaturals. She is depicted as wearing a white mask with a red spot on each cheek, a small beard, and a red tongue hanging from a mouth which has prominent teeth.

She has ear pendants, and a red feather is attached to the crown of her head. There is a fox skin about her neck, and she is clothed in a white blanket, tied with a knotted girdle.

POWAMÛ

(Plates XIV and XXII)

On the morning of the last day of the Powamû festival there are dances in the kivas in which participate unmasked men called Powamû katcinas, a figure of one of whom is given in the accompanying plate.

---

[a] For a description of these, see Journal of American Folk-Lore, vol. VI, 1893.

[b] The Hano name, Imbesaiya, which is applied to Yohozro wüqti, means grandmother, possibly the Snow katcina's grandmother.

PLATE XXII

NÜVAK

YOHOZRO WÜQTI   POWAMÛ

PLATE XXIII

WUKOKOTI

KOHONINO

These men wear in their hair a number of artificial flowers, made of painted corn shucks. The bodies of these men are painted, but otherwise they wear no distinctive dress or paraphernalia.

WUKOKOTI

(Plate XXIII)

This figure of Wukokoti (Big Head) has a black face with protruding snout, two lateral horns, and prominent globular eyes. The artist represents one of two beings who roam through the pueblos in the March festival, hooting wherever they go. It is one of many beings of the same name who appear in the February and March festivals. The personators carry bundles of sheep scapulæ, which in late years have been substituted for those of deer.

KOHONINO

(Plate XXIII)

This figure [a] represents a katcina derived from the Havasupai (or Kohonino) Indians engaged in animated conversation with a man of the same tribe.

The mask has a headband, on each side of which is a horn wrapped with red and black calico. The marks crossing the headband also represent variegated cloth.

Two eagle feathers arise from the head, and to the top of the feathers are attached red balls representing fruit of the prickly pear.

The chin is crossed by oblique bands, colored red and blue, and the mouth is triangular in shape. Two red spots, one on each cheek, complete the symbolism of the picture.

The accompanying figure representing a Havasupai Indian is unmasked, and shows several characteristic marks. He has a headband, from which rises a hoop, to which are attached two eagle feathers, with a fragment of red cloth in the rear. The coat and leggings, like Kohonino garments, are buckskin, and there is fringe on the latter.

TCOSBUCI AND SOYAN EP

(Plate XXIV)

The main figure is said to have been derived from a Yuman tribe, as the Walapai, who formerly wore turquoise (tcosbuci) nose ornaments. The artist has represented Tcosbuci and Soyan ep fencing with arrows.

The symbolic mark of the former is an hourglass design. The face is painted green, the eyes are of brown color with green border. The hair is tied Yuma fashion behind the head. The red ring in the middle of the face represents a turquoise.

---

[a] For picture of the doll, see Internationales Archiv für Ethnographie, Band VII, fig. 15.

Tcosbuci has black bands painted on the left arm and right leg. He wears a black kilt under a buckskin shirt, and has a quiver with arrows. The bow is carried in one hand.

Soyan ep has a black mask with feathers on his head, lozenge-shaped eyes, and small goatee. Both legs and arms are striped with black bands. His shirt is made of buckskin.

NAKIATCOP

(Plate XXIV)

The figure of Nakiatcop has a crest of eagle feathers on the head, and in most respects resembles the Dawn katcina. The mask used in personating this being is said to belong to the Badger clan.

KOKOPELLI

(Plate XXV)

The Hopi call a certain dipterous insect kokopelli and apply the same name to a personation said to have been introduced by the Asa clan.

The head is painted black and has a white median facial line. The snout is long, pointed, and striped in spiral black and white. On each side of the head is a white circle with diametrical lines drawn in black, and there is a warrior feather on top.

The body is black, and girt by an embroidered sash. There are buckskin leggings, stained yellow and green. A hump is always found on the back in pictures or dolls of Kokopelli.

The author has been informed that in old times many of these beings appeared at the same time, but he has never seen the personation.

KOKOPELLI MANA

(Plate XXV)

The Kokopelli girl has a slender, protuberant snout painted with spiral lines. She carries in her hand two packets[a] of food made of mush wrapped in corn husks.

LAPÜKTI[b]

(Plate XXV)

The symbolic marks of Lapükti are three parallel marks on each cheek, hair of cedar bark, long telescopic eyes, and a protuberant snout. He carries a rattle in his right hand, a crook in the left, and wears shirt and pantaloons. The picture brings out all these characteristics.

---

[a] Somipiki.

[b] For picture of doll, see Internationales Archiv für Ethnographie, Band VII, pl. XI, fig. 40.

PLATE XXIV

TCOSBUCI AND SOYAN EP

NAKIATCOP

PLATE XXV

KOKOPELLI

KOKOPELLI MANA

LAPÜKTI

PALÜLÜKOÑTI (AÑKWAÑTI) FESTIVAL

MACIBOL

(Plate XXVI)

These two figures represent masked men who sometimes appear in the March festival (Añkwañti) carrying effigies of the Great Serpent, with which they appear to struggle, twisting them about their bodies and causing them to make various gyrations in a startling manner.

One of the arms represented in the picture is a false one, which is hung on the shoulder of the performer, the real arm being hidden in the body of the serpent effigy. The man holds the stick which is the backbone of the serpent with the hidden hand and with it imparts the wonderfully realistic movements to the serpent.

Each figure wears a buckskin blanket and a mask painted green, across which is a black zigzag band rimmed with white, which in form resembles the snake symbol on the kilt of the Snake priests. The helmet has two horns and a bunch of feathers on the top.

The backs of the two serpent effigies differ in color, one being black and the other brown, but the bellies of both are white. The triangular symbols on them represent bird tracks; the double parallel marks represent feathers.

Their heads have a fan-shaped crest of feathers, a median horn curving forward, and a necklace of feathered strings. The eyes are prominent, and the teeth and tongue are colored red.

Macibol is another name for Calako, the sun god, and the episode here figured represents the sky god wielding the lightning.

PALÜLÜKOÑ AND TATCÜKTI

(Plate XXVI)

There are many rites in the Añkwañti in which the effigies of Palülükoñ, the Great Snake, play an instructive rôle. This picture represents the struggle of a clown with one of these effigies, as personated in the March mystery drama.

The effigy is made to rise from a jar on the floor to the ceiling, and when it is thus extended a clown steps up to it and appears to struggle with it; he is finally overcome. There are modifications of this drama which call for special description,[a] but none of these are represented in the collection of pictures.

FIGURINES OF CORN MAIDENS

(Plate XXVII)

On certain years there is introduced in the Hopi mystery drama, Añkwañti, an interesting marionette performance which is illustrated by this picture. The Honani or Badger clan of Sichumovi have two

---

[a] See A Theatrical Performance at Walpi, Proceedings Washington Academy of Science, vol. II, 1900, pages 605–629, and pages 40–55 of this paper.

figurines representing the Corn maidens, which were made by a man named Totci, who now lives at Zuñi. These figurines and a framework or upright with which they are used are shown in this picture, which represents the figures kneeling before a miniature grinding stone placed on the floor.

As the symbolism has been explained in a description of Calako mana, it need not be redescribed, but it may be well to note that the dotted bodies appearing on these figurines below the kilt represent the feathered garment which this maid and some other mythical personages are said to wear.[a]

The designs on the framework symbolize rain clouds and falling rain. During the mystery play the two bird effigies are made to move back and forth on the framework by a man concealed behind the screen, who also imitates bird cries.

The two figurines are manipulated by means of strings and other mechanical oliances. Their arms are jointed, and as a song is sung the marionett s are made to imitate meal grinding, raising their hands at intervals from the meal stones to their faces.

TACAB AÑYA AND MANA

(Plate XXVII)

This picture represents a being called Navaho Añya katcina, and his sister, who grinds corn ceremonially in the kivas on the final night of the Añkwañti. The attitude of the girl is that assumed by her after the corn has been ground, when she and her sister dance and posture their bodies before a line of Añya katcina personators serving as a chorus.

The masks of the Navaho Añyas are similar to those of the Hopi, except that the former have terraced figures or rain-cloud symbols in each lower corner, and a red instead of a black beard. The male wears a red kilt, tied by a belt of silver disks, which are common Navaho ornaments.

The dress of the girl consists of a black velvet shirt and a red calico skirt, with a piece of calico over her shoulders. She wears a Navaho necklace.

Her coiffure is a cue tied behind the head, like that of the Navahos. The projecting lip, illustrating a habit of gesticulating with the lower jaw so common among Navahos, is common in Hopi pictures of these Indians.

OWANOZROZRO

(Plate XXVIII)

This being appears in the Añkwañti, going from kiva to kiva beating on the hatchways and calling down to the inmates. The

---

[a] Fabrics obtained in cliff houses and other old Arizona ruins show that it is probable that cloth in which feathers were woven was worn by the ancient ancestors of the Hopis.

PLATE XXVI

MACIBOL

PALÜLÜKOÑ AND TATCÜKTI

PLATE XXVII

FIGURINES OF CORN MAIDENS

TACAB AÑA AND MANA

PLATE XXVIII

OWANOZROZRO

COTO (WALPI)

COTO (ORAIBI)

PLATE XXIX

HOPAK AND MANA

KOKYAN WÜQTI   PÜÜKOÑ KATCINA

picture represents him beating a stone with a yucca whip. The mask
is colored white, and has a projecting mouth, goggle eyes, two horns,
and a mass of hair. The part of stone beater is now taken by boys,
and the two personators seen in 1900 stood at the kiva entrances
striking the ladder and raised hatchway, calling down the kiva entrance
as if angry. They wore loose blankets and no ceremonial kilts.

COTO

(Plate XXVIII)

There are two pictures of Coto, the Star katcina, one representing the Walpi, the other the Oraibi variant; the masks of both are
readily distinguished from all others by the arrangement of the star
symbols.

The East mesa or Walpi Star katcina has three vertical stars
attached to the top of the masks, a star painted on the right cheek,
and a half-moon on the left. There are also star figures on the forearms and legs. Four feathers are represented on top of the mask
and others hang from the elbows. There are yucca whips in the
hands. The kilt has a radiating turkey tail feather covering, which
has a unique form.

The whole face of the Oraibi Star katcina is covered by a single
star. It has a string of feathers extending down the back and a collar
of spruce twigs. The body is painted yellow and black and the arms
and legs have longitudinal bands.

The garments are painted red, and in the left hand is carried a
yucca whip, in the right a bell. Red color appears to characterize
all the paraphernalia.

HOPAK AND MANA

(Plate XXIX)

One of the katcinas which appeared in the Añkwañti was called
Hopak (hopoko, eastern), and evidently derives its name from the
fact that it came from eastern pueblos. Hopak was accompanied by
a girl being, evidently his sister (civaadta).

The distinguishing symbolism is the triangular mouth and the
zigzag markings around the face, which is painted green. The hair
of the girl is dressed in the same way as that of the Zuñis and the
Pueblo women of the Rio Grande. Small rectangles in two colors are
painted on each cheek. The girl was called sister of the Püükoñ katcina when he appeared in the Añkwañti.

KOKYAN WÜQTI[a]

(Plate XXIX)

When the Püükoñ katcinas danced in the Añkwañti there accompanied the dancers a personation called So wüqti, Grandmother woman, and as the grandmother of Püükoñ is Kokyan wüqti (Spider woman), So wüqti is supposed to be another name for this being.

The mask is perfectly black, with yellow crescentic eyes and white hair. She wears a dark-blue blanket, over which is a white ceremonial blanket with rain-cloud and butterfly symbols. She carries a sprig of pine in each hand.

PÜÜKOÑ KATCINA

(Plate XXIX)

The picture of Püükoñ katcina[b] has a black mask surmounted by a netted war bonnet, with two eagle tail feathers attached to the apex. There is a small conical extension on top of this bonnet, the usual distinguishing feature of the lesser war god.

The figure has a white blanket about the body which is painted black, and wears a white kilt with rain clouds embroidered on the margins. The hose are made of an open-worked netted cotton fabric. In the left hand there is a bow and arrow, and in the right is the ancient war implement, a stone tied by a buckskin to the extremity of a stick.[c]

PÜÜKOÑ HOYA

(Plate XXX)

The face of Püükoñ hoya bears the customary parallel vertical marks, and on the head is a war bonnet with apical extension and warrior feathers. He wears on his back a quiver of mountain-lion skin, and carries a bow and arrow in his left hand, the symbolic lightning framework, with feathers attached at the angles, in the right. The white marks on body, legs, and arms shown in the picture are characteristic. The reader's attention is called to the similarity of the symbols of this picture to those of Püükoñ katcina.

PALUÑA HOYA

(Plate XXX)

Paluña hoya, the twin brother of Püükoñ hoya, has a mask with a protuberant snout, but does not wear a war bonnet. He has, like

---

[a] The part was taken by Nanahe, a Hopi who lives in Zuñi and who had returned to Walpi for that purpose.

[b] For picture of the doll, see Internationales Archiv für Ethnographie, Band VII, pl. v, fig. 59.

[c] One of these implements can be seen on the altar of the Kalektaka in the Momtcita ceremony.

PLATE XXX

PÜÜKOÑ HOYA

PALUÑA HOYA

TCANAÛ

TUCKUBOT

PLATE XXXI

WUPAMAU

MUCAIAS TAKA

MUCAIAS MANA

his brother, two vertical marks on each cheek, which, however, are black instead of white, and the warrior feather on his head. He carries a whizzer in the right hand and a bow and arrows in his left, and wears a bandoleer across his left shoulder. His body and extremities are painted brown and black.

TCUKUBOT

(Plate XXX)

This is one of the numerous horned katcinas, distinguished by a black helmet, white goggle eyes, and two bands across the face. They roam about through the pueblos in certain great festivals.

TCANAÛ

(Plate XXX)

Tcanaû is an instructive personage. The picture represents him as he appears in the Añkwañti.

The mask is flat and has eagle feathers and two sticks similar to those of the Wupamau mask radiating from the margin. The brown bodies between these radiating eagle feathers are also feathers, a bunch of which covers the back of the helmet.[a]

The face is destitute of symbolic markings, but a stuffed image of a snake hangs from the mouth.

Tcanaû carries a slat of wood and a meal bag resembling that of the Snake priests in his left hand, and in his right a crooked stick. Four of these beings appeared in the Añkwañti, and the personation is said to have been originally introduced into Tusayan by the Pakab clan.

WUPAMAU

(Plate XXXI)

This picture[b] represents a being the mask of which has a symbolism recalling that of the sun. The face is flat, and is divided into three regions by a horizontal and a vertical line. One of the lateral regions is yellow, the other is green. The chin is black and there is a long snout slightly curved downward, with an appended piece of leather, colored red, representing the tongue.

Around the rim of this face, more especially the upper part, is a plaited corn-husk border, in which are inserted at intervals three prominent eagle feathers and numerous smaller feathers. The latter are but portions of a mass which cover the whole back of the helmet.

When Wupamau appears in Powamû or Añkwañti, he is accom-

---

a The masks seen in the Añkwañti have carved wooden lizards attached to their foreheads.

b For picture of the doll, see Internationales Archiv für Ethnographie, Band VII, pl. VI, fig. 6.

panied by a clown carrying a lasso, which in the picture is fastened around the body of the katcina.

There are masks of Wupamau in all three villages of the East mesa, and these are all worn in the Añkwañti ceremony.

MUCAIAS TAKA

(Plate XXXI)

The Buffalo youth, as represented in the picture, has a face painted black, with white crescents indicating eyes and mouth. Over his head is a blackened wig made of a sheepskin, which also hangs down his back, replacing the buffalo skin, which was always used when this animal was abundant. To each side of the head covering is attached a horn with appended eagle feathers. Across the forehead is an embroidered fabric like those used for katcina heel bands.[a]

The kilt of the Buffalo youth is white, with red and black stripes along the edges; it is tied by a string to which shells are attached. A large cotton belt is now generally used for a girdle.

In his left hand the Buffalo youth carries a zigzag stick, representing lightning, to each end of which feathers are attached. In his right hand he has a rattle decorated with stars.[b]

MUCAIAS MANA

(Plate XXXI)

This picture represents the Buffalo maid, who appears in the Mucaiasti, or Buffalo dance, with the youth mentioned above. She is unmasked, but wears hanging down over her forehead before the eyes a fringe of black hair tied to a string about her forehead. On the crown of her head there is a bunch of parrot and eagle breast feathers. A wooden stick, to one end of which is attached a symbolic squash blossom and to the other two eagle tail feathers, is placed horizontally over the crown of the head. This squash blossom is made of yarn stretched over radiating spines. Two black parallel lines are painted on each cheek, and she wears a profusion of necklaces and three white cotton blankets. About her body, tied under her left arm, is a ceremonial dance kilt, the embroidered decorations representing rain clouds and falling rain.

The two other blankets, one of which is tied over her right shoulder, the other about her loins, bear on the embroidered rim rain-cloud and butterfly decorations. She has white leggings, embroidered anklets, and white moccasins. The blanket is bound to

---

[a] In old times these bands were made of porcupine quills, but these are now rare and are replaced by embroidered worsted of different colors.

[b] A very good doll of Mucaias taka, made for the author in 1900, has patches of white on the body, arms, and legs, and the kilt is tied by a miniature white girdle.

her loins by a great cotton belt, the ends of which are shown on the left side.

In each hand she carries a notched prayer-stick, called a sun ladder, which is painted yellow on one side of the median line, green on the other.[a]

On her back the Buffalo maid wears a sun symbol, which, divested of the peripheral eagle feathers, the artist has shown to the right of the picture. The tips of these feathers are shown on each side of the arms; the accompanying lines represent stained horsehair.

AÑYA KATCINA MANAS GRINDING CORN

(Plate XXXII)

In several ceremonies, especially those in the kivas which dramatize the growth of corn, there is a ceremonial corn grinding, which also sometimes occurs in the public plazas, as is illustrated by this picture. The figures of the group are as follows:

1. Two Añya katcina manas
2. Two Hehea katcinas
3. Four Añya katcinas
4. One Paiakyamû

All these figures have symbolic masks which have elsewhere been described as characteristic.

It will be noticed that the two whorls of the girls' hair are different from those generally worn by Hopi maids. This particular form is said to represent a very ancient coiffure, which is made by winding the hair over an hourglass-shaped piece of wood, but this object is not removed, as are the curved sticks commonly used in making the whorls.

The sequence of events in this ceremonial corn grinding is as follows: The two Heheas first enter the kiva or plaza, bearing on their backs two metates or grinding stones done up in sheepskins, which they place side by side. Narrow boards, decorated with rain clouds and bird figures, are set up about them, and a plaque of meal, with a brush, is placed by their side. The Heheas, having arranged these objects, seat themselves on each side of the grinding stones in the attitude shown in the picture. The masked girls then enter and take their positions by the metates.

A line of thirty or more Añya katcinas, of which only four are shown in the picture, then file in and take their positions back of the maids; with them enters the Paiakyamû, or glutton, who seats himself facing the girls.

After an interlocution between the Heheas and the kiva chief, who sits by the fireplace facing them, the trend of their conversation being that the girls are clever meal grinders, the chorus begins a

---

[a] The artist has made a mistake in painting both sides green.

song, accompanied by a dance, while the girls grind the meal and the Heheas clap their hands. After a short time the Heheas take some of the meal from the grinding stones and carry it to the kiva chief or to the clown, and put it in his mouth to show its excellence. They respond that it is good, and the Heheas resume their seats, shouting and clapping their hands as before.

After a little while the Heheas take more of the meal and thrust it into the mouths of the other spectators for them to taste, all the time carrying on a bantering conversation with the chief. After this proceeds for some time the girls rise, the metates are brushed, done up in the sheepskins, and laid at one side. The girls then stand in front of the line of Añya katcinas and posture their bodies, holding ears of corn in the hands, which they extend one after another in the attitudes shown in the picture of Alo mana.

The being called Añya katcina, while apparently very old among the Hopis, resembles the Zuñi Kokokci in both symbolism and general character, which suggests that both may have been derived from a common source. It is not improbable that this source in both instances was the pueblos of the Patki clans, the ruins of which are situated on the Little Colorado river.

It is interesting in this connection to note that the whorls of hair of the Añya manas more nearly resemble those of the Zuñi personations of girls than those of the Hopi, which, so far as it goes, tells in favor of a common derivation.

HOKYAÑA

(Plate XXXIII)

The figure of Hokyaña katcina is accompanied by that of a drummer. He wears a bearded maskette colored green and has hair cut in terraces across the forehead and below the ears, but hanging down the back. This way of cutting the hair in terraces is symbolic of rain clouds.

There is a bunch of feathers on top of the head, and a string with attached feathers hangs down the back. The lower rim of the maskette has alternate blocks of red, green, white, and black colors, as in Añya katcina masks. One side of the body is painted red, the other blue.

The drummer is dressed like a Navaho, with calico or silk headband, velvet trousers, buckskin leggings with silver buttons, and belt of silver disks.

Hokyaña is said to be distinguished from Añya by his peculiar step in dancing.

PLATE XXXII

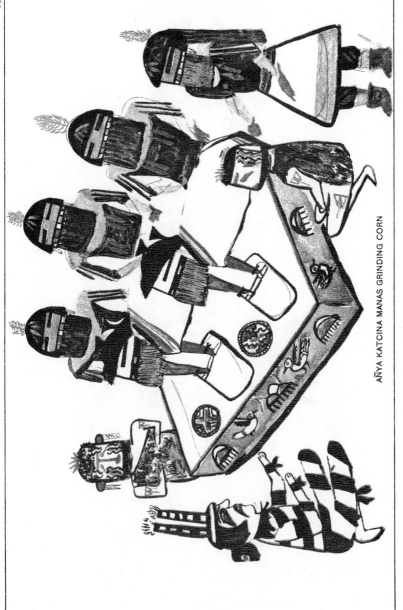

AÑYA KATCINA MANAS GRINDING CORN

PLATE XXXIII

HOKYAÑA

HOKYAÑA AND MAÑA

HOKYAÑA MANA

(Plate XXXIII)

The maid or sister of the preceding, as figured by the Hopi artist, has her hair dressed in Zuñi fashion and carries an ear of corn in each hand.

CAKWAHONAÛ

(Plate LXIII)

The collection of katcina pictures would have been increased several fold were we to include in it many which are duplicates in all respects save color. It may be borne in mind that while almost all these beings have yellow, green, red, and white variants, as a rule only one color is drawn. This is true of the present picture representing the Green Bear; but we have also the yellow, red, and black bear with the same general symbolism.

The distinguishing symbolism of the Bear katcina are bear paws, one on each cheek, which are at times difficult to distinguish from those of the Badger. It has a prominent snout, and a visor on the helmet, to which lightning symbols and feathers are attached.

KOKLE

(Plate XXXIV)

The artist represents in this picture the symbolism of Kokle, and depicts an episode when this person bears a deer on his back.

The facial markings of the mask of Kokle represent a cornstalk medially placed, extending over the eyes.

Kokle is a very common design on the interior of modern bowls, where the head only is generally represented.

CITOTO

(Plate XXXIV)

The mask of Citoto is conical or half ovoid, with semicircular alternating parallel bands of red, yellow, green, and black on each side. The mouth has the form of a curved beak, at the base of which is attached a fringe of red horsehair. A cluster of variegated parrot feathers is attached to the back and apex of the mask. Citoto carries a rattle in his right, a pine tree in his left hand.

There are two Citoto helmets on the East mesa. One of these hangs in a back room of Anote's house (Sa clan, Hano), the other is in the special keeping of the Walpi Pakab clan, which also claims, in addition to Citoto, masks of Sabi (Tcanaû), Tanik, and Türkwinû, male and female. The Tanik helmet closely resembles Wupamau, and Türkwinû (Mountaineer) is so called from the San Francisco Mountain people, which would indicate that it was derived from some of the people who once lived along the Little Colorado.

Sumaikoli Ceremony

SUMAIKOLI AND YAYA

(Plate XXXIV)

This picture represents a Sumaikoli led by a Yaya priest, as they appear in two festivals each year, one in the spring, the other in summer. New fire is kindled by frictional methods in the former and is carried by means of a cedar-bark torch to shrines of the fire god at the four cardinal points. In abbreviated presentations the masks are left in the kiva, where they are arranged in a row with that of Kawikoli, and the men who carry the fire are unmasked and not accompanied by a Yaya priest. The Sumaikoli are supposed to be blind, and eyes in the masks are mere pin holes, so that when they are worn a guide is necessary.

There are six masks of Sumaikoli and one of Kawikoli in Walpi and Hano which differ slightly in colors and symbolism, but the accompanying figure gives a fair idea of one of the Sumaikolis.

It will be noted that the figure wears the same embroidered sash on the head that is seen in the picture of Masanû, and that the appendages to the leggings are the same shell tinklers which are prescribed for sun gods.

KAWIKOLI

(Plate XXXV)

The picture of Kawikoli represents a being with a globular mask painted black, having two white marks on each cheek. A bundle of feathered strings is tied to each side, and the skin of a mountain lion surrounds the neck. The chin has red and green curved bands inclosing a white area. The figure is represented as carrying fire in a cedar-bark torch from one shrine to another, accompanied by a Yaya priest, who has a rattle in his right hand and an unknown object in the left. The kilt is tied behind and has draperies of colored yarn.

The mask of Kawikoli is displayed with those of Sumaikoli in the festivals of these personages. Kawikoli is also personated at Zuñi, from which pueblo the name was probably derived.

CIWIKOLI

(Plate XXXV)

The picture of Ciwikoli represents a being with mask painted brownish red, having two parallel white lines on each cheek. There are tadpole figures on the sides of the mask and a fan-shaped feather appendage to the top of the head.

PLATE XXXIV

KOKLE

CITOTO

SUMAIKOLI AND YAYA

PLATE XXXV

KAWIKOLI

CIWIKOLI

TACAB (NAACTADJI)

Ciwikoli wears a kilt made of red-stained horsehair, and a bandoleer. He carries a whizzer or bull roarer in his right hand. A fox skin is tied about his neck.

Ciwikoli is a Zuñi personation. Words like Sumaikoli, Kawikoli, Ciwikoli, having the termination -koli, are foreign to the Hopi language, although common in eastern pueblo tongues.

NAVAHO KATCINAS

TACAB (NAACTADJI)

(Plate XXXV)

This Navaho god is incorporated in the East mesa ritual, and is known by the following characteristic symbolism:

The mask has a projecting visor, to the rim of which is attached a row of eagle feathers inserted vertically in a wad of straw, the edge of which shows above the visor. A conical structure made of sticks colored red, tipped with yarn, red horsehair, and eagle feathers arises from the top of the head.

One side of the face is colored green, the other red, the two sides being separated by a white median band, across which are parallel black lines. The eyes are represented by horizontal bands painted black. The pointed marks above and below the eye slits, with which they are parallel, represent gourd sprouts. A symbolic squash blossom is appended to each side of the helmet. This object is made of wood or a section of a gourd, and is crossed on the concave face by diametrical lines, at the point of intersection of which there is an eagle feather. The right side of the body and corresponding arm are colored yellow, the left red. A network of red lines covers the body, as is indicated in the picture.

The bandoleer and necklace are pine boughs, which are also carried in the hands. Two eagle feathers are tied to each armlet. The belt is composed of silver disks, and the kilt is colored red and white; the latter has green diagonals, and tassels on the lower corners. Sleigh bells are attached to a garter of yarn tied below the knee.

TACAB (TENEBIDJI)

(Plate XXXVI)

The artist has figured in this plate one of the most common Navaho katcinas personated by the Hopis. The eyes are black, horizontal bands, curved at the outer ends; the snout is long. On that side of the head which is turned to the observer there is a symbol of a half-formed squash surrounded by red horsehair, and to the opposite side of the head are attached two vertical eagle feathers. On the crown of the head are variegated parrot feathers. The red fringe on the forehead represents the hair.

TACAB (YEBITCAI)
(Plate XXXVI)

The name of this Navaho supernatural is translated Grandfather katcina, and the Hopis say that the Navaho name has a like meaning. The artist has depicted on the mask a stalk of corn on a white face. The eyes and mouth are surrounded by two half rectangles. A conventional ear of corn is painted on the left cheek. There is likewise a crest of eagle feathers on the head. Yebitcai wears a blue calico shirt, black velvet pantaloons, and Navaho leggings. Both the pantaloons and the leggings have a row of white disks along the outside which represent the well-known silver buttons, and he wears a belt of silver disks strung on a leather strap. A buckskin is represented over his right shoulder, and in his left hand he carries a bow and two arrows, and a skin pouch for sacred meal.

TACAB
(Plate XXXVI)

The artist has also represented another Navaho katcina with points of symbolism similar to that of Yebitcai. The face is painted white, with crescents under the eyes and mouth. There is a representation of a stalk of growing corn on the median line of the mask, and an ear of maize on each side.

The figure wears a red kilt and a black bandoleer, and carries yucca whips in his hands.

SOYOHIM KATCINAS

Under this name the Hopis include many masked personages which appear in dances called by the same name (called here also Abbreviated Katcina dances).

KAE
(Plate XXXVI)

Very few of the Hopis identified the picture of this katcina as Kae or Corn katcina, the name given to it by the artist. The validity of this identification is supported by the predominance of the maize symbol, which covers the whole back of the mask.

To the rear lower part of the head are attached feathers, two of which are vertically placed. The right side of the face is painted green, and on it are markings representing sprouting corn seeds. The visor has wooden slats, symbolic of lightning, tied to its rim.

On one side of the picture the artist has represented the ordinary triple rain-cloud symbol above a corn plant, and some of the Hopis said that the rain-cloud design should have been painted on all the pictures in the collection.

PLATE XXXVI

TACAB (TENEBIDJI)

TACAB (YEBITCAI)

TACAB

KAE KATCINA

PLATE XXXVII

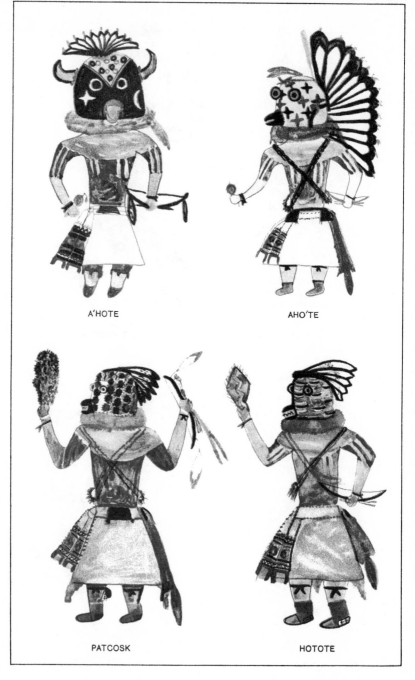

A'HOTE

AHO'TE

PATCOSK

HOTOTE

AHO'TE

(Plate XXXVII)

Two pictures, both called Ahote, from the cry uttered by the personator, differ widely from each other in symbolism. The name of one has the accent on the penult, that of the other on the antepenult.

Aho'te has a helmet painted yellow, with goggle eyes, a prominent snout, and face covered with red and black four-pointed stars. The figure has two bandoleers, a white kilt with pendent fox skin, and an embroidered sash. A large string of eagle feathers hangs down the back.

A'HOTE

(Plate XXXVII)

A'hote has a black helmet with great goggle eyes and a single four-pointed star on the right cheek, a new moon on the left. Unlike Aho'te, he has two horns, one on each side of the head, and a triangle on the forehead painted yellow, in which are black and red rings. On the head there is a small fanlike feather appendage.

TÜRTUMSI

(Plate LXII)

The picture of Türtumsi represents a goggle-eyed katcina with yellow mask, on which are parallel rows of black lines extending longitudinally. The figure has a black beard, to which are fastened two cotton strings. A row of eagle feathers is attached to the head and hangs down the back, as shown in the picture, and there is a rattle in the right hand, a bow and arrows in the left.

Several Hopis gave the name Komantci (Comanche) to this katcina. Possibly it was derived from this tribe, with which the ancient Hopis were familiar.

PATCOSK

(Plate XXXVII)

This characteristic being is readily distinguished by the cactus on the head and in the hand. He also carries a bow and arrows.

HOTOTO

(Plate XXXVII)

Hototo katcina has crescentic marks painted green and red on the face, goggle-eyes, and a short snout. In his right hand he carries an object on which appears the zigzag lightning symbol.

The Hopis say that Hototo is so named from the cry "Hototo, hototo!" which the personator utters.

KEME

(Plate XXXVIII)

The drawing of Keme katcina has slanting bands of yellow, green, and red across the middle of the face, which is painted green, with terraced figures in red and yellow in two diagonal corners. The top of the head, as represented, is flat, and to it are appended bunches of parrot and turkey feathers, two of which project on each side.

The dress and other paraphernalia of Keme katcina are in no respect distinctive.

SIWAP

(Plate XXXVIII)

Siwap katcina has a black helmet with a prominent globular snout, green eyes, and a triangular, green-colored figure on the forehead. The necklace is made of corn husks, a few of which are also tucked into the belt. The kilt is black, and there is an antelope horn in each hand.

HOTCANI

(Plate XXXVIII)

The symbolic markings of this being are clearly brought out by the Hopi artist in his picture.

The face is painted green, crossed by a black band with red border. On the top of the head are radiating feathers and parrot plumes. Pine boughs are inserted in the armlets and belt, and there are branches of the same tree about the neck. The kilt is white, without decoration, and the sashes are embroidered.

From the linguistic similarity of the name Hotcani to Hotcäuni of the Sia, mentioned by Mrs Stevenson, they are regarded as identical. The Hopi variant is probably derived from the Keresan.

TAWA

(Plate XXXVIII)

The Sun katcina has a disk-shaped mask, which is divided by a horizontal black band into two regions, the upper being subdivided into two smaller portions by a median vertical line. The left lateral upper division is red, the right yellow, the former being surrounded by a yellow and black border, the latter by a red and black. In the lower half of the face, which is green, appear lines representing eyes, and a double triangle of hourglass shape representing the mouth.

Around the border of the mask is represented a plaited corn husk, in which radiating eagle feathers are inserted. A string with attached red horsehair is tied around the rim or margin of the disk.

PLATE XXXVIII

KEME   HOTCANI

SIWAP   TAWA

PLATE XXXIX

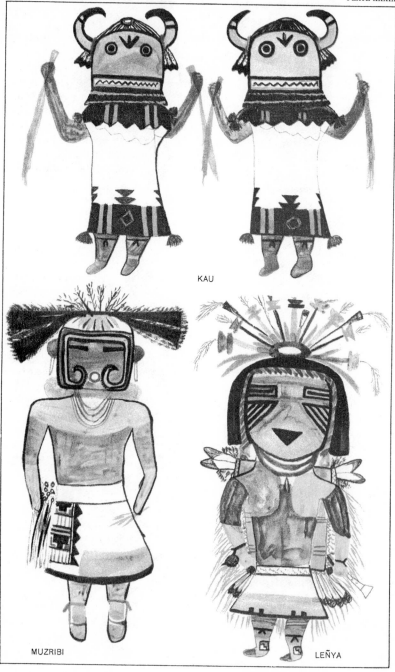

KAU

MUZRIBI

LEÑYA

In his left hand Tawa carries the flute which is associated with him in certain Hopi solar myths.[a]

It will be found that this type of sun symbolism is to be easily detected in various katcinas of different names which have been mentioned, and it is more than probable that many of these, possessing the same, or nearly the same, symbolic markings, are sun gods under different names. This multitude of sun gods is readily explained by the composite nature of the present Hopi people, for each clan formerly had its own sun god, which, when the clan joined Walpi, was added to the existing mythological system. The type of symbolism has persisted, thus revealing their identity.

KAU

(Plate XXXIX)

This katcina is readily recognized by the two horns and dependent crest of feathers on the head, the characteristic mouth, and short beard. The two figures here given differ from each other in their colors—one being green, the other yellow. Both have characteristic triangular symbols on the forehead.

MUZRIBI

(Plate XXXIX)

The picture of Muzribi, the Bean katcina, has on each side of the mouth, or snout, the sprouting seed of a bean. The face is bordered by yellow and red marginal lines which are continued into the curved markings, representing bean sprouts, on the cheeks.

There are four horizontally-placed feathers on the top of the head, and a bunch of smaller feathers at their attachment.

LEÑYA

(Plate XXXIX)

Leñya, the Flute katcina, as shown in the picture, has a green face with rectangular eyes, the left colored yellow bordered with black, the right blue with the same colored border. There are chevrons of black lines on the cheeks; the mouth is triangular in form.

Attached to the crown of the head there is an annulet made of corn husk painted green, in which are inserted artificial flowers and feathers.

Leñya wears on the back a tablet made of skin stretched over a rectangular frame, the edge of which is shown on each side of the

---

[a] There are many published pictures of the Hopi symbolic sun disk. See Fifteenth Annual Report of the Bureau of American Ethnology, 1897, pl. CIV; American Anthropologist, vol. X, 1897, pl. II, figs. 36, 37, 40, pl. IV, fig. 112; Journal of American Folk-Lore, vol. VI, 1893, pl. I; Proceedings Washington Academy of Science, vol. II, 1900, pl. XXXII.

neck and body.   The dentate markings on the visible edge represent
a plaited corn husk border, and the appended red marks represent
horsehair.   The two objects extended horizontally on the upper
corners are eagle feathers arising from a cluster of feathers at their
attachment.

Leñya carries a flute in his left, a rattle in his right hand.

PAÑWÛ [a]

(Plate XL)

Pañwû, the Mountain Sheep katcina, is represented by two figures,
one of which wears a kilt tied with great cotton girdle, shirt, and
leggings, while the other is naked.   The heads of these two figures
are practically identical, both having two imitations of sheep horns,
along which are drawn zigzag lines in green color, representing lightning.   The mask has a protuberant visor, from which hang turkey
tail feathers.   The snout is prominent, and there are artificial squash
blossoms on the sides of the head.   The naked figure has the back
and sides of the body and outside of the limbs painted blue or green,
with the abdominal region white.   Attention is called to the peculiar
unknown bodies inserted into armlets and garters.

The other picture of this katcina has the same symbols on the mask,
but the figure wears a buckskin shirt and fringed leggings.   A white
kilt with red and black borders is tied about the loins by a great
cotton girdle, and a semicircular framework with attached feathers
is carried on the back.

TIWENU

(Plate XL)

The picture representing Tiwenu has a tablet on the head, the
upper rim of which has a terrace form representing rain clouds.   On
the sides of the face are pictures of symbolic corn ears of different colors, that on the left representing white corn, that on the right, green
corn.   The semicircle painted on the tablet represents a rainbow above
a white field in which is a four-pointed star.

The eye slits are painted black, with a white margin.   The lower
part of the face is black, the chin white.   There is a projecting snout,
with teeth and red lips.   The figure carries a pine branch in each
hand.

KOROCTÛ

(Plate LXI)

This is a Keresan katcina, as its name [b] signifies.   The picture
represents a plain mask with a white or black arrowhead figure for

---

[a] For picture of the doll, see Internationales Archiv für Ethnographie, Band VII, pl. VII, fig. 14.

[b] Akorosta.   The words sung by Koroctû are Keresan, as is the case with those sung by several
other katcinas of eastern origin.

PAÑWÛ

TIWENU   KWEWÛ

PLATE XL

PLATE XLI

TCÜB   CIPOMĔLI

SOWIÑWÛ

mouth and two horizontal black marks with upturned ends for eyes. The face is green, with red, yellow, and black border; the ears have pendants of corn husks. The blanket is white, with embroidered border.

Each figure carries in one hand a skin pouch with sacred meal, and in the other a rattle or a number of deer scapulæ.

KWEWÛ [a]

(Plate XL)

The picture representing the Wolf katcina has a well-drawn wolf's head with projecting mouth, and a wolf's paw, painted black, on each cheek. To the tips of the ears are appended feathers, stained red, and there are eagle feathers on the side of the head.

The kilt is made of horsehair, stained red, hanging from a belt which supports the breechclout. The legs and forearms are spotted. Kwewû is generally personated with the Antelope and Deer katcinas running back and forth along the line of dancers, assuming the posture represented in the drawing.

TCÜB [b]

(Plate XLI)

The picture of Tcüb, the Antelope katcina, represents a being with two antelope horns on top of the head, an hourglass design in black on the face, black spots on each cheek, and a bunch of feathers, from which arise two eagle tail feathers, on the back of the head. The mask has a long protuberant snout and an artificial squash blossom on each side.

The bodily decoration and dress are in no respect characteristic. In the hand there is a staff, to the top of which feathers are attached. The symbolism of Tcüb katcina is very close to that of Sowiñwû.

SOWIÑWÛ

(Plate XLI)

In the three pictures of Sowiñwû the artist has represented two Deer katcinas ascribed to the old pueblo Awatobi, and with them a deer hunter of that pueblo, the tradition of whom is still told at Walpi.

The Deer katcinas have green helmets with projecting visors, from which hang rows of turkey feathers. Deer horns are attached to the top of the head and two eagle tail feathers project from the back. There is an hourglass design in black on the middle of the face and a black dot on each cheek. A circle with radial lines, denoting the six cardinal points, is painted on each side of the mask.

---

[a] For picture of the doll, see Internationales Archiv für Ethnographie, Band VII, pl. V, fig. 2.
[b] For picture of the doll, see same volume, pl. VII, fig. 13.

The hunter has the chevron symbolic of the eagle over the nose and wears a kilt of red horsehair. He wears a bandoleer and a netted shirt. In his right hand he carries a rattle, in his left a bow and arrows.

The author has obtained the following legend regarding the deer hunter: An Awatobi maid gave birth to a child, which she hid in a cleft in the mesa side. Isauû (Coyote) found this babe and carried it in her mouth to Tcübio wüqti, the Antelope woman, who lived in Awatobi. Tcübio wüqti had milk and brought up the child, who became a celebrated hunter of antelopes.

The Sowiñwû katcina has not been personated of late years by the Walpi men, but there is good authority for the statement that it has been represented within a few years by the Mishongnovi people. At the period of the destruction of Awatobi many of the clans went to the Middle mesa and one or two of the Awatobi cults are still more vigorous there than elsewhere.

CIPOMELLI

(Plate XLI)

The figure represents an ancient katcina peculiar to the pueblo Hano, but now rarely personated.

TUMAE

(Plate XLII)

The picture of this katcina has a face divided into a yellow and green section by a vertical black line. The lower part of the face is separated from both by a horizontal black line, and is colored red. In the middle of this red zone there is a rectangular chin painted white, the pigment which gives the name to the figure. Both Hopis and Tewas call this katcina Tumae (white earth), referring to the white pigment on the chin.

MATIA

(Plate XLII)

This figure has a human hand painted on the face, on which account it is called Matia, or Hand katcina. Another designation, Talakin, refers to the girl who follows, stirring the contents of a cooking pot which Matia carries on his back. He is said to appear in the foot races, but the author has never seen him personated at Walpi.

A being with the figure of a hand on the face occurs also in Zuñi dances.

PLATE XLII

TUMAE

MATIA

PLATE XLIII

PIOKOT

TÜRKWINÛ   TÜRKWINÛ MANA

PIOKOT

(Plate XLIII)

The pictures of this katcina have a circle of various colors on the forehead and red club-shaped bodies on the cheeks. The figures wear embroidered sashes on their shoulders—an unusual position for these objects—and tight-fitting black kilts, tied above with green belts. Evidently the distinguishing symbols of Piokot are the diagonal club-shaped marks on the cheeks, for two other pictures of Piokot, by a different artist, have neither the variegated circle on the forehead nor the embroidered scarf about the neck.

TÜRKWINÛ

(Plate XLIII)

This figure has an undecorated mask with a row of parallel marks, symbolic of falling rain, on the upper edge, where there are likewise three semicircular figures representing rain clouds. A row of turkey feathers is drawn before the face. The hair and beard are represented by pine boughs. It carries a ceremonial water gourd in each hand and wears a simple white kilt with green border, decorated with red-colored rain-cloud symbols.

The name (türkwi) indicates that this katcina was derived from some mountain pueblo. The Tewas give the same name (Pompin) to it that they give to the San Francisco mountains. One of the best traditionists has said that this katcina was derived from people who once lived in the foothills of these mountains.

TÜRKWINÛ MANA

(Plate XLIII)

The maid or sister of Türkwinû has a headdress in the form of a terraced tablet, upon which semicircular rain-cloud symbols are painted. She likewise has pine boughs representing hair.

Her face is divided by a median band, with parallel horizontal black lines, into two parts, the left side being painted brown and the right painted white. There are semicircular lines about the mouth. She wears a white blanket bound by a great cotton belt, has turkey feathers tied to the blanket, and carries a cake in her hand.

TOHO

(Plate LXIII)

Toho, the Puma, wears a mask of green color, with a projecting snout armed with teeth. Eagle feathers are attached to a string hanging down the back, and there are parrot feathers in the hair.

The body has yellow parallel bars on breast, arms, and legs. The kilt is of horsehair stained red, and in each hand is a whip made of yucca wands.

KUTCA

(Plate XLIV)

Kutca, White katcina, has a white mask with two parallel vertical black marks on each cheek and a mouth of triangular shape.

There is a horn tipped with an eagle feather attached to the left side of his head; its proximal and distal extremities are connected by a string, to which is tied red horsehair. A sunflower symbol is depicted on his forehead, and there are eagle and parrot feathers on top of his head. He carries a bow in the left hand and a bundle of sheep scapulæ in the right, and wears over a spotted (calico) shirt a white cotton blanket decorated with butterfly and rain-cloud symbols. On his back is a mountain-lion's skin.

KUTCA MANA

(Plate XLIV)

The sister (mana)[a] of the preceding has, like her brother, a white mask with two parallel black marks on each cheek. The hourglass bodies on each side of the head represent whorls of hair, but are made of corn husks.

ÛRCICIMÛ

(Plate XLIV)

This figure has a green mask, with projecting snout, arising from a fringe of sheepskin stained red. The eyes are protuberant and colored yellow. There are colored feathers on the crown of the head and two eagle feathers at the back. The paw of an animal is depicted on each cheek. The figure is clothed in a rabbit-skin rug, girt with a belt, has naked feet, and wears a pair of red horsehair anklets. The wands in the hands are of cactus, and to their ends roasted ears of corn are tied.

YEHOHO

(Plate XLIV)

The left cheek of Yehoho is colored yellow, the right red; they are separated by a black band. The eyes are curved at the corners, and on the head there are two horns. The necklace is made of pine boughs.

This katcina wears a rabbit-skin rug and an embroidered belt, and across the body there are two bandoleers formed of ears of roasted corn tied in strings. He holds an ear of the same in each hand.

The garment worn by Yehoho is called tokotcpatcuba, and the corn on the bandoleers is called takpabu.

---

[a] Mana literally means maid.

PLATE XLIV

KUTCA

KUTCA MANA

YEHOHO

ÜRCICIMÛ

PLATE XLV

SIO

SIO

SIO MANA AND THREE KOYIMSI

ZUÑI KATCINAS

SIO

(Plate XLV)

The Zuñi katcina[a] has designs on the face which recall the solar symbols. The upper part is divided by a vertical line into two regions, one red and the other green (blue in the picture), the right-hand side being bordered by yellow and green, the left-hand side by red and spotted bands. The remaining or lower part of the face is colored green; the left eye is painted yellow. There is a long, slim, yellow, protuberant snout. A symbolic squash is appended to the right side of the helmet, and two vertical eagle feathers are tied to the left side. There are likewise indications of a fan-like crest of eagle feathers on the top of the helmet and a cluster of highly colored feathers at the point of attachment of the two vertical eagle feathers.

SIO MANA AND THREE KOYIMSI

(Plate XLV)

In this picture the Zuñi maid and three mudheads are represented as they appear in an East mesa ceremony.

The maid wears a maskette like that of Añya mana, and holds aloft in one hand a badge of office, which among the Zuñis is beautifully formed of parrot feathers. In her other hand she carries a clay basket or sacred meal receptacle. Her headdress is Zuñi rather than Hopi.

The figures of the Koyimsi are characteristic, each wearing a helmet with cloth knobs full of seeds. Two of these beings, who wear small fawn skin bandoleers, hold aloft rattles, and one has a drum, which he is represented as beating with the characteristic Zuñi drumstick.

CITULILÜ

(Plate XLVI)

The significance of the Zuñi name Citulilü[b] is shown at once by the rattlesnake on the forehead.

The two pictures of Citulilü differ only in the color of the mask and of the snake on it. One has a yellow, the other a black face; the snake on the former is green, that on the latter is brown.

The fan-shaped crest over the helmet is made of turkey tail feathers and the red mass represents painted wool. The snout is long and protuberant, with a red tongue made of leather.

---

[a] For description of dance called by this name, see Journal of American Ethnology and Archæology, vol. II, 1892.

[b] Cetola, a Zuñi word for rattlesnake.

The costuming of Citulilü is similar to that of the Hopi Snake priests, although the body, save the forearms and legs, is not painted red, but black. He wears an armlet to which are fastened strips of buckskin, dyed red. The bandoleer is also stained red. The kilt, like that of Snake priests, is painted red, and upon it is drawn a zigzag design representing the Great Plumed Snake, with alternating white bars and angular designs. The green bands above and below represent rainbows. The sash is of buckskin, stained red. The heel bands have the same color and are made of horsehair. Citulilü carries a yucca whip in each hand.

There is said to be also a red, white, and green Citulilü katcina.

TEÜK

(Plate XLVI)

The picture of this katcina was identified by most of the Hopis as that of a Sio or Zuñi katcina. The symbolism of the mask is similar to that of Tacab katcina, with which it is sometimes confounded.

PAKWABI

(Plate XLVI)

The picture of Pakwabi represents a warrior. He wears a war bonnet made of buckskin, with perforations and an apex tipped with a feather. Four archaic rain-cloud symbols are painted around the lower rim.

The face is black, the eyes are white, the snout is long and project-ing, the hair is done up in a queue down the back. The blue covering of the body is of calico, over which is thrown a buckskin. A bandoleer is worn over the left shoulder and the kilt has Navaho silver disks.

The pantaloons and leggings are likewise Navaho, the former velvet, with rows of silver buttons. In his right hand Pakwabi carries a whizzer, ornamented with a zigzag lightning symbol, and in his left are a bow and arrows.

The name is evidently from some place or pueblo from which the personage was derived. If so, the name of that pueblo may have been derived from pakwa (frog), obi (place).

KWACUS ALEK TAKA AND ALO MANA

(Plate XLVII)

The picture of Kwacus Alek taka has a green mask with red back and two eagle tail feathers resembling horns, one on each side.

Alo mana, the sister of Alek taka, has a white maskette with artificial wig and feathers dependent from the lower rim. She is represented in the characteristic attitude assumed in her dance.

PLATE XLVI

CITULILÜ

TEÜK

PAKWABI

PLATE XLVII

KWACUS ALEK TAKA

ALO MANA

OLD MASK (KATCINA CLAN)

OLD MASK (TCÜA CLAN)

Both these beings are said to be of Zuñi origin and the latter was formerly personated by a man from Hano. The characteristic attitude of Alo mana is also taken by the girls after the ceremonial corn grinding elsewhere described.

ANCIENT CLAN MASKS

In the back rooms and dark corners of most of the important clans of the pueblos of the East mesa masks will be found hanging to the roof beams, the use of which has almost wholly been abandoned. The distinctive names of these masks are difficult to obtain, and they are generally known by such designations as Wüwükoti, ancient masks or heads. The chiefs of the clans ordinarily claim them as their particular property, and other men of the pueblo who are familiar with their existence usually call them by the names of the chiefs.

Some of these old masks are brought forth from time to time, renovated, and put to use; others are never worn, but are carefully preserved with reverence befitting their antiquity, for the majority are reputed to be very ancient.

It is probable that some of these masks, dingy with age and rarely or never repainted, have come into the possession of the present owners at the death of the last members of kindred clans. Others have been passed down directly from chief to chief, still remaining in keeping of the clan which brought them into the country, and may be regarded as among the more ancient of Hopi masks. Unfortunately the knowledge of their characteristic symbols has in some instances been lost.

There are also individual masks which have not the special sanctity that pertains to the above. These were introduced from other pueblos by visitors or by those who had observed them elsewhere in their trading or other trips. These are not regularly used each year, but may be brought out on special occasions for variety or other reasons. They are associated with the man who introduced them, and often bear his name.

There is a general similarity in these old clan helmets, both in form and in symbolism, which would seem to refer them to a group by themselves. Among the common features may be mentioned the two horns, the radiating eagle feathers, red horsehair, and the markings on the face. Thus the clan mask of Kotka (Bear chief) is almost identical with that of Wiki (Snake chief), and both resemble that of Naka (Katcina chief). Evidently they are not totemic of the clan, or at least their symbols are not characteristic of the clan, but their similarity implies that they are symbolic of some common personations for which they were once used.

Of all the masks now employed in personations the author regards the old clan masks as nearest in symbolic designs to those of Calako, and it is possible that they were used in representing the same beings for which Calako masks are still employed. The author believes that the Calako giants are personations of sun gods and that the ancient clan masks of the Hopi are survivals of those once used in sun personations by extinct or nearly extinct clans. The former use of these masks in sun worship and their antiquity give them a particular sanctity; the chiefs rarely use them, but preserve them with great reverence.

Objection might be made to this identification, for these clan masks have two horns, which are absent in Hopi sun masks, and the facial markings are different. The author theoretically connects the horns with those of the bison, and believes that the clans which once had these forms of sun masks derived them from those tribes which practiced a Buffalo sun ceremony.

OLD MASK (KATCINA CLAN)

(Plate XLVII)

This ancient mask is called Naka's katcina from the name of the chief in whose keeping it now is, and probably belonged to an old Katcina clan. The picture represents a disk-formed head, painted green, with goggle eyes. The upper half of the head is surrounded by a plaited corn-husk border, with inserted eagle feathers forming a crest, in which are red lines, indicating horsehair. On each side of the head are represented horns, decorated with zigzag marks, which are repeated on the forehead.

The mask which is here figured is not now used, but hangs in a back room of the house of the Katcina clan. It is said to have been brought from Kicyuba, the ancient pueblo of this clan. Probably the clan of which it was the sun mask is now extinct, and the mask remains in the keeping of the chief of the clan nearest related to that which once owned it. The sun mask of the Katcina clan, called Ahül or Old Man Sun, is elsewhere described.

OLD MASK (TCÜA CLAN)

(Plate XLVII)

The ancient mask of the Tcüa or Snake clan, called Wiki's katcina, in whose keeping as clan chief it is, has a rounded top, with bearded face surrounded by a plaited corn-husk border in which are inserted radiating eagle feathers and red horsehair.

A horn is appended to each side of the head, and between the eyes on the forehead appears an arrow symbol. The body is painted red and the kilt is horsehair of the same color.

OLD MASK (HONAU CLAN)

(Plate XLVIII)

The ancient mask of the Honau or Bear clan is called Kotka's katcina, and is in the keeping of this chief. The Bear people were the first to arrive at Walpi, and their last village before they came there was situated at Türkinobi, on the mesa above Sikyatki, where the ruins of their old home are still pointed out. Kotka belongs to the Spider (Kokyan) clan of the Honau phratry, and is not only chief but also the sole remaining male member of this ancient Hopi family.

The similarity of the mask to other old helmets is striking. The edge of the face is surrounded by plaited corn husks in which are inserted eagle tail feathers forming the crest. The red marks represent red horsehair. The two horns are commonly found with Wüwükoti masks, and the beard is not an uncommon feature. The red object protruding from the mouth represents a tongue.

POHAHA (TE CLAN)

(Plate XLVIII)

This picture represents a katcina called Pohaha by the Tewas, Nalucala by the Hopis, the mask of which is owned by Wehe, a member of the Te clan. The propriety of the name Nalucala (four horns) appears from the picture. The face is divided as in other sun masks, and there is a hideous mouth and beard. In the right hand the figure carries a whizzer or bull-roarer, and in the left a bow and arrows. It wears a bandoleer on the shoulder, over which is thrown a buckskin.

The leggings remind one of those worn by the eastern or Plains Indians, with whom the Tewas were formerly connected. This is undoubtedly one of the katcinas which the Tewa colonists brought to the East mesa in early times.

HOPIÑYÛ (ISAUÛ CLAN)

(Plate XLVIII)

This picture represents an ancient personage of the Isauû (Coyote) clan, and is commonly known as Lesu's katcina, from the fact that the mask used in personating it is in the keeping of this man, who is the clan chief.

The face is divided by a median vertical line into two fields, one colored white, the other green. The lower part of the face, separated from the upper by a horizontal line, is colored red, and there is a long, pointed snout. Both sides of the face are covered with small crosses or stars.

A row of eagle feathers is continued from the head down the back, with red lines shown among the feathers, indicating horsehair. There are highly colored parrot feathers on the top of the head.

Accompanying the figure of Hopiñyû, the artist has drawn a picture of Samo wüqtaka (Old Man Cactus), who carries a cactus fruit in one hand and a basket of the same on his back.

Hopiñyû is sometimes called a Sikyatki katcina, as the clan by which the helmet is now owned formerly lived in a pueblo near Sikyatki, called Kükütcomo, which is now a ruin. The author has seen a fragment of pottery from Sikyatki, on which is drawn a face identical in symbolism with that which is here depicted as characteristic of Hopiñyû.[a]

KE TOWA BISENA

(Plate LXII)

This ancient mask belongs to the Bear family of Hano, and has a general similarity to Kotka's[b] mask, or that of the Honau (Bear) family of Walpi.

There are the same radiating eagle feathers about the head, the lozenge-shaped eyes, mouth, and long beard, but no horns are represented in the picture. In place of the latter we have, on the right-hand side, a symbolic squash blossom, and on the left, feathers.

The katcina, as represented, has a fox skin about the neck and a bear skin over the shoulders. He carries a ceremonial water gourd in the right hand, a small pine tree in the left. The artist has also represented two bear paws on the feet.

MASKS INTRODUCED BY INDIVIDUALS

SIO (SOYOWA)

(Plate XLV)

A Hopi named Wikyatiwa[c] introduced a few years ago into Walpi from Zuñi a katcina to which the name Soyowa has been given. The picture of this being shows a mask with two upright tablets, one on each side, terraced to symbolize rain clouds. On the front of the lower part of these tablets there are symbolic sunflower symbols, and the visor of the mask has the form of a crest of eagle feathers. Two figures painted on the forehead are rain-cloud symbols. The face is green, with three oblique lines, colored yellow, red, and blue, on each cheek. The introduction of this katcina by a man still living at Walpi is an instructive example of the way in which additions have been made to the Hopi pantheon in modern times.

---

[a] The etymology of this word is doubtful, but there can be detected in it a likeness to the word hopoko (eastern), referring, no doubt, to its origin from eastern pueblos, from which the Sikyatki clans are reputed to have come.

[b] Kotka really belongs to the Spider clan, which all regard as one of the Bear group.

[c] Wikyatiwa is a member of the Walpi Snake clan.

PLATE XLVIII

OLD MASK (HONAU CLAN)

POHAHA (TE CLAN)

HOPIÑYÛ (ISAUÛ CLAN)

SAMO WÜQTAKA

PLATE XLIX

YUÑA

YUÑA MANA

WAKAC

MAKTO

YUÑA [a]

(Plate XLIX)

The Cactus katcina, introduced by Homovi, has not been personated for many years. On the head are drawn branches of the so-called prickly-pear cactus, the red berries of which are realistically shown.

The symbols of the helmet are the moon and stars on a white field, and similar stars appear on the breast and forearms. Elaborate armlets with suspended feathers are shown near the shoulders, and a bow and arrows are represented in the left hand. To the former, feathers of the eagle are attached. The collar is of pine branches, and sprigs from the same tree are inserted in the armlets and belt.

YUÑA MANA

(Plate XLIX)

The Cactus maid who accompanies the Cactus katcina carries a pair of cactus tongs, an implement made of wood by which the prickly pear is gathered, in her right hand, and in her left a basket or bowl containing the fruit. She wears a mask painted white with two vertical black marks on each cheek. She has likewise turquoise ear pendants, triangular mouth, and hair arranged in two whorls above the ears.

WAKAC [b]

(Plate XLIX)

The Cow katcina mask, commonly named after Satele, a Hano man of the Bear clan who introduced it, has a cow's head, realistically drawn, but with no distinctive symbolic markings.

MAKTO [c]

(Plate XLIX)

The mask represented in this picture has the figure of a putckohu, or rabbit stick, across the face. It has likewise two parallel marks on each cheek, and carries rabbit sticks, one of which is raised as if in the act of being thrown. There are two rabbit sticks in the left hand. Pontima, chief of the Ala clan, owns the mask, and it is commonly called his katcina.

PAKIOKWIK

(Plate LXII)

Pakiokwik, the Fish katcina, was introduced into Hano by a man named Kanu. A design representing a fish is depicted on the face.

---

[a] From the Spanish tuna, prickly pear.

[b] Evidently from Spanish vaca, cow. The Hopi word wakac means cow.

[c] This name is derived from the circle which rabbit hunters make when they hunt these animals: makto, hunt.

This is an excellent example, of which there are many, serving to show how a man who in recent years has seen an object which he believed to be efficacious in bringing rain, has made a picture of it on his mask.

PERSONATORS APPEARING IN RACES CALLED WAWAC

Several masked men are introduced by the Hopis in their foot races, which are elsewhere[a] described. A Hopi foot race is conducted as follows: A half dozen men representing clowns wearing masks take position in line at one end of the plaza behind a blanket placed on the ground, upon which are the prizes—corn, dried peaches, and paper-bread. They challenge the spectators to run for these prizes, and any-one who wishes to do so steps before the blanket, and immediately the race is on, the course being generally across the plaza.

The clown or masked man carries a whip or sheep shears, and if he overtakes the contestant he strikes him vigorously with the whip, or in some cases cuts off his hair. If, however, the spectator who has accepted the challenge outruns the masked man, the prize which was announced before starting belongs to him.

These races often occur in the midst of katcina dances, and clowns and other masked individuals participate in them to amuse the spectators.

In pictures of Wawac the Hopi artist has as a rule represented the prizes, generally a string of paper-bread (piki), hanging above the picture.

AYA

(Plate L)

This katcina appears in pairs in the Wawac, or Racing Katcina, and is readily recognized by the rattle (aya), which has swastika deco-rations on both sides, forming the head. The snout is seen in the blue projection near the left hand.

Aya wears the belt in a peculiar way, the ends hanging in front and behind, not on one side as is usually the case.

The red objects above the pictures represent rolls of paper-bread, the prizes in the races.

LETOTOBI

(Plate L)

The two figures represented in this picture have the characteristic attitude of runners; they appear in the Wawac, as the prizes hanging above them indicate. Their masks have characteristic red bands across the mouths and eyes, and are surmounted by crests of yellow fox skins. Their bodies are smeared black.

---

[a] A Tusayan Foot Race, Bulletin Essex Institute, vol. XXIV, 1892, p. 113–136.

PLATE L

AYA

LETOTOBI

RACER   HEMICO

PLATE LI

TCUKAPELLI

KONA

PALABIKUÑA

TCILIKOMATO

MACMAHOLA

HEMICO

(Plate L)

The picture represents an Indian pursued by the dreaded katcina called Hemico.[a] The bundle of paper-bread and a few ears of roasted corn which hang above them are prizes.

Hemico has in his hand a pair of sheep shears, with which, if he overtakes his opponent in the race, he cuts off his hair. In his right hand he carries a yucca whip, with which he also flogs his opponent. Other characteristic symbols of this being are parallel bands of color across the forehead, and ring figures of various colors dependent from a yellow band around the top.

Hemico is said to have been derived from Sikyatki, and it is recounted in legends still preserved that he cut a Walpi girl's throat with a stone knife, the deed which ultimately led to an attack on Sikyatki by the Walpians and the destruction of that pueblo.

TCUKAPELLI

(Plate LI)

These two beings, one of whom wears a peculiar mask, represent episodes sometimes introduced during katcina dances as a byplay to amuse spectators. In this instance one of the Tcukapellis[b] has under his left arm a bag full of clay balls, one of which he holds in his right hand in the attitude of throwing it at his companion. The other has four tufts of hair fastened to the top of his head. The bodies are naked, save for a breechclout, and are smeared with mud.

PALABIKUÑA

(Plate LI)

This katcina appears in the Wawac, as is indicated by the rolls of paper-bread hanging above the figure. He wears a red kilt,[c] which gives him his name, and carries yucca wands in his hands with which he flogs the naked runners in the races if he overtakes them. The objects on the sides of the head are frameworks of sticks.

KONA

(Plate LI)

Kona, the Chipmunk katcina, likewise appears in the Wawac, as the prizes of yellow and red paper-bread hanging above the figure

---

[a] The word hemico is applied to the queue in which the Hopi men tie their hair behind their heads.

[b] Mud ball (tcuka) thrower.

[c] Pala, red, pitkone, kilt.

indicate and the yucca whips in his hands imply. The mask represents the head of the chipmunk, and the body is painted in parallel stripes to make the resemblance even more realistic.

MACMAHOLA

(Plate LI)

This being sometimes takes part in the foot races. The picture shows a globular mask, two sausage-like appendages on the top of the head, and an old planting stick in one hand.

TCILIKOMATO

(Plate LI)

This picture represents a hunting katcina, with rabbit sticks (putckohu) in both hands. There are two vertical black marks on each cheek and two horns on the head. Tcilikomato is personated in foot races.

WIKTCINA

(Plate LII)

This being assists the clowns, and amuses the spectators by throwing mud during the dances and festivals.

PIPTUKA[a]

(Plate LII)

Piptuka appears in public dances and is a participant in the antics of the mudheads, or clowns. He carries a hoe over his shoulder and a planting stick in his left hand, indicating his connection with planting.

PATUÑ

(Plate LII)

Patuñ, the Squash katcina, is represented as a man with body painted green with black stripes, bearing squash blossoms in his hands. The mask is of the same green color, with black stripes, and is made of a large gourd bearing an imitation of a squash flower on the larger end.

TATACMÛ

(Plate LIII)

These two figures are playing a game which is sometimes introduced in katcina dances. This game consists mainly in striking a buckskin ball with a stick. Each person holds the end of a string attached to this ball, which flies back and forth as struck by the players.

---

a See Journal of American Ethnology and Archæology, vol. II, 1892, p. 82, 155.

PLATE LII

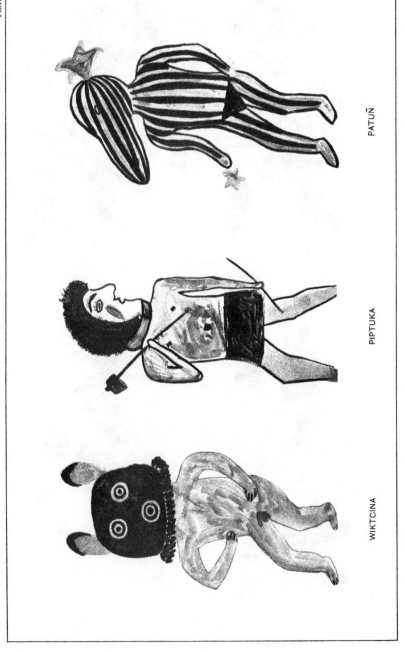

WIKTCINA PIPTUKA PATUÑ

PLATE LIII

TATACMÛ

PASKI

They wear masks which have nose, eyebrows, and mouth represented in relief. The eyes have black radiating lines, and there is a
black zone on the lower edge of the mask. The hair is a fragment of
sheepskin painted black, and there are several feathers on the head.
Each player has eagle tail feathers tied to his shoulders.

PASKI

(Plate LIII)

These pictures of Paski represent a planting katcina. An examination of the masks shows one with red and green parallel lines on the
cheeks, the other with a broad red band. One has the hair done up
in a queue behind; the other has it hanging down the back. Both
wear black belts on their loins and have white kilts thrown over the
shoulders in a peculiar way. They are represented as using modern
hoes.[a]

NAKOPAN PERSONAGES

(Plate LIV)

A short distance from the ruin of Sikyatki there is a cave in the
side of the mesa concerning which there is a well-known tradition
preserved to our time. It seems that when Sikyatki was in its prime
two children left their home and lived in this cave hidden from their
mother. Their hiding place, at first unknown to their parent, was
afterward discovered, and their mother daily brought them food and
laid it on the rocks above the cave. The children used to go to this
place to obtain the food, and a pictograph still visible there marks the
place where they sat.

The author was anxious to get a picture of the Nakopan hoya, or
the Nakopan children, as they are called, and this plate drawn by a
Hopi named Winuta is the result. The following personages are
depicted in the picture:

a, Telavai or Dawn katcina; *b*, Hahai wüqti; *c*, Mana, maid; *d*,
Paiakyamû; *e*, Hehea katcina; *f*, Añya katcina; *g*, Tatcükti.

On account of the illicit love of Hahai wüqti and Paiakyamû,
who are represented arm in arm, Telavai, her husband, sought the
maid, whose arms he grasps. Hehea, Añya, and possibly Tatcükti,
the children, fled from Sikyatki and lived in a neighboring cave.

This picture, so far as the evidence goes, supports the belief that
the Sikyatki people were familiar with the katcina cult; and it is
instructive to notice that it portrays some of the most ancient katcinas
of the Hopis.

---

[a] In old times a planting stick was employed.

BEINGS NOT CALLED KATCINAS

LAKONE MANA

(Plate LV)

The two maids represented in this picture appear in the basket dance called the Lalakoñti. The bands on their heads support rain-cloud symbols, and to these bands are attached horns and squash-blossom symbols. The objects rising vertically from the back of the heads and the clusters in the same place represent eagle tail feathers.

The faces of the girls are painted yellow, with black bands across the temples and from each corner of the mouth to the ears. In their hands they carry half corncobs with two appended eagle feathers, which objects are thrown into figures of rain clouds made of meal on the ground by their male companion, called Lakone taka.

The dress of Lakone mana, especially the appendages to the head-band, differs somewhat in the different Hopi pueblos, as may be seen by consulting a description of the basket dances.[a]

MAMZRAU MANA

(Plate LV)

These pictures represent the two girls who appear in the Maraupaki or Mamzrauti, an October festival, in which the women carry in their hands wooden tablets bearing figures of corn and rain clouds, and other designs.

The thighs of the personators are painted with black rectangles, and on the heads there are wooden frameworks with apical eagle feathers and red horsehair. They wear kilts reaching nearly to the knees, the only instance to the author's knowledge of the use of this garment by girls in ceremonial dances. Their hair is tied down the back.

PALAHIKO MANA

(Plate LVI)

This figure represents Palahiko mana as she appears in the Mamz-rauti ceremony. The head tablet is tied by a string under the chin, and to this tablet is attached a band which passes over the forehead, as shown in the picture. The tablet is made of flat boards, and con-sists of six parts, two vertical, two lateral, and two diagonal, each representing rain-cloud symbols tipped by eagle feathers.

The red objects, one on each side between the lateral and vertical components of the tablet, are symbolic squash blossoms, or the whorls in which Hopi maidens dress their hair. The cup-shaped, pedunculated

---

[a] Journal of American Folk-Lore, vol. XII, 1899, p. 81-96.

PLATE LIV

NAKOPAN PERSONAGES

PLATE LV

LAKONE MANA

MAMZRAU MANA

PLATE LVI

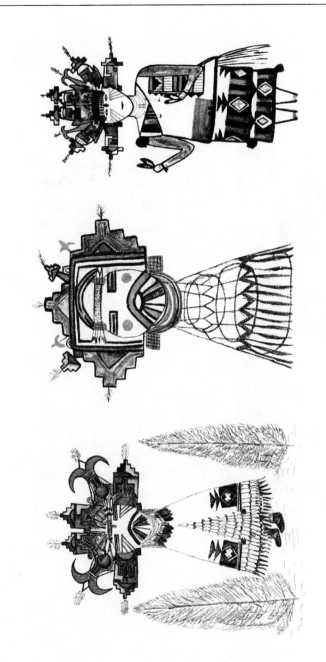

HOPI CALAKO MANA   HOPI CALAKO MANA   PALAHIKO MANA

PLATE LVII

BULI MANA

objects in the hair represent corn flowers. The band across the forehead marked with bars represents an ear of corn, and the red bodies attached to· each end are fragments of sheepskin, symbols of corn tassels. Two eagle tail feathers also are attached to each end of the symbolic corn ear. The median object, colored green, hanging between the eyes, represents a fragment of Haliotis shell.

Red chevrons are painted on the face. The square, green pendants, one on each side of the head, represent turquoise ear pendants, which are highly prized by the Hopi maidens.

Palahiko mana[a] wears three blankets—a kilt, thrown across the right shoulder and hanging under the left arm, with rain-cloud and falling-rain designs embroidered on it, and two wedding blankets, with triangular rain-cloud and butterfly symbols, tied about the body. The ends of the great white girdle are shown under the upper of these blankets on the left side. The necklace is of coral beads, and strings of turquoise pendants are shown about the neck. The figure carries a feathered stick in each hand.

HOPI CALAKO MANA

(Plate LVI)

On one of the two pictures of this being is seen a mask with a prominent tablet almost identical with that of the preceding. The tablet represents terraced rain clouds, of which there are two vertical and two horizontal, one of each on each side. The object with bifid tips on each side of the tablet represents the squash blossom, symbolic of maidens' hair dress.

Across the forehead is a symbol of an ear of corn, with two feathers attached to each end. The ring hanging over the forehead represents a fragment of Haliotis shell. There are imitation flowers made of wood represented in the hair. The left eye is yellow, the right blue. The chevrons on the cheek are similar to those found on the face of Palahiko mana.[b]

The artist has represented a garment of feathers, over which is thrown a white ceremonial blanket with embroidered border. The two adjacent trees are pines.

BULI MANA

(Plate LVII)

Buli mana, the Butterfly maid, appears in a dance which was introduced from the Rio Grande pueblos, where it is called the "Tablita," from the tablets worn by the women on their heads. This dance is

---

[a] For picture of doll, see Internationales Archiv für Ethnographie, Band VII, pl. IX, X, fig. 28, 31; Fifteenth Annual Report of the Bureau of American Ethnology, 1897, pl. CVII, CIX, fig. 39.

[b] These beings, Palahiko mana and Calako mana, probably represent the same conception.

occasionally performed at the East mesa, but is unaccompanied by secret rites.

Each figure bears on the head a board tablet, the edge of which is cut into terraces representing rain clouds. Figures of sunflowers or the sun, or other symbols are painted on these tablets.

Although the personator of this maid is without a mask, her cheeks are painted with red spots. The blue or the yellow garment, as the case may be, is made of calico, under which is a woman's blanket, bound to the waist by a red belt.

The small figure between the two girls represents the standard bearer, who precedes a procession composed of men and women alternating with each other, the latter being dressed as in the pictures. The standard bearer carries a long pole, to the top of which is attached a gourd, painted black, with red-stained horsehair and parrot and other feathers attached. In the few representations of the Butterfly dance which have been given in late years, this standard bearer has carried a banneret on which is painted a picture of a Hopi girl.

COTOKINUÑWÛ

(Plate LVIII)

This picture represents Cotokinuñwû, the Heart-of-the-sky god, who is readily recognized by the single curved horn on the head and the rain-cloud symbols on the face and base of the horn.

In his left hand he carries the framework of sticks which symbolizes the lightning. This framework has attached to each angle an eagle feather, which the painter has indicated in black lines.

In the right hand he carries the whizzer or bull-roarer, a slat to which a string is attached, with lightning represented by a zigzag band in red. Two bandoleers are represented. The legs and forearms are painted black.[a]

KAISALE

(Plate LVIII)

This picture was identified by all as Kaisale, the name given it by the artist.

KAISALE MANA

(Plate LVIII)

This picture represents a maid accompanied by a Hano glutton (Paiakyamû). The former holds an ear of corn aloft, as in the dance called Klahewe which is celebrated at Zuñi.

---

[a] The symbol of the Sky god is sometimes an equal-armed cross. Other symbols are lightning designs or figures of plumed snakes.

PLATE LVIII

COTOKINUÑWÛ

KAISALE

PAIAKYAMÛ

KAISALE MANA

PLATE LIX

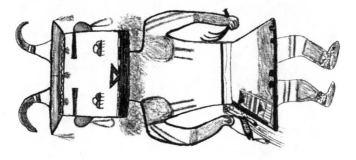

ALOSAKA

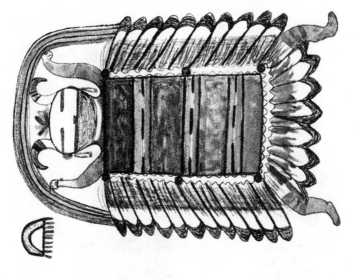

ALOSAKA

ALOSAKA

(Plate LIX)

Two pictures of Alosaka were drawn by the Hopi artist. One of these has a mask with two short, curved horns, such as novices wear in the Aaltû society. In the left hand this Alosaka carries a deer horn, and in the right a representation of a badge (moñkohu) made of a slat of wood.[a]

The second picture of Alosaka[b] is more elaborate than the first. It has the two horns on the head, and the chin is painted black. The semicircular figure above the head represents the rainbow on which gods are said to travel; it is appropriately introduced with Alosaka, who is said to have walked on it from the San Francisco mountains to meet an Awatobi maid.

A great part of the picture is taken up by a large rectangular figure of a moisture tablet (pavaoakaci), an object worn on the back by many personators. This tablet is, strictly speaking, a framework over which is stretched cloth or buckskin, painted as indicated in the figure.[c] The zigzag lines about the border represent plaited corn husks, in which feathers are inserted. The red lines drawn between these feathers represent red horsehair, and the small circular objects, three in number on each side, are small disks made of gourds.

AHÜLANI[d]

(Plate LX)

This figure represents the Soyal katcina, Ahülani, and the two Soyal manas as they appear on the morning of the last day (Totokya) of Soyaluña, as elsewhere described. The decoration of the Ahülani mask differs in its symbolism on alternate years, accordingly as the Snake or the Flute dance is celebrated. In the latter case the eyes and mouth are represented by crescentic marks, but in the former we find a horizontal black band across the face through the eyes.

Ahülani carries under his left arm several ears of corn, and spruce boughs or twigs. In his left hand he bears a chief's badge and skin pouch with sacred meal, while in his right he carries a staff.

The two Soyal manas differ only in the color of the corn which they carry; one has yellow, the other blue corn. Each has a yellow maskette, before which falls a bang composed of horsehair stained red. An eagle breast feather is fastened to the scalp. The lower

---

[a] For figure of moñkohus, see description of the New-fire ceremony, where personations of Alosaka appear, American Anthropologist, new series, vol. II, 1900, p. 90.

[b] The name Alosaka is the Awatobi name of the germ god, the Sikyatki equivalent being Masauû and Eototo, and the general name Muyiñwû.

[c] Morphologically a sun emblem or "back shield" representing the sun.

[d] The returning one, i. e., the sun god.

part of the mask is banded green, red, and black, and black feathers are attached to its lower border. In their hands the maids carry basket plaques, on which are rings of corn ears set on end, with cedar boughs, here represented green. In the white inclosed space formed by this ring of corn ears is raw cotton.

In the Walpi winter solstice festival, the three beings here represented emerged from the kiva at dawn, and sang at different points in the pueblo, after which they retired to the kiva and distributed seed corn to the women of the village.[a]

The similarity of the words Ahülani and Ahül is explained by a derivation of both from the word ahülti (return). The Ahül katcina is the Return katcina, the first in Powamû to return to the pueblo. He is in fact the Tawa wüqtaka (Old Man Sun), and the similarity of the symbolism of his mask to that of the sun is evident. So Ahülani is the "return katcina making," or the returning sun of the Patki, as Ahül is the returning sun of the Katcina clan. Both these names are attributal names of the sun.

Although Ahülani, as his picture shows, has no sun symbolism in his mask, his crescent eyes are often seen in sun symbols. There is another indication that he may be in some way connected with the sun. A personation of Ahül katcina is said to appear in some of the other pueblos in place of Ahülani, which substitution indicates their identity. In the dance in the kiva the night before Ahülani and the Soyal manas appear, there is a man representing a bird which the author interprets as a personation of the sun;[b] the Soyal manas are regarded as either germ goddesses or cultus heroines of the Water-house or Raincloud clan. In kiva exercises the personation of the sun takes an eagle form, which is not assumed in public, although the same god is personated in the plaza under the name Ahülani.

TANOAN NAMES FOR HOPI KATCINAS

In the following list are given the Hano (Tanoan) names of about sixty of the personages figured in the preceding pages. Many of these are simply Tanoan translations of the Hopi names, a few names are identical with the Hopi, and a large number are entirely different.

In the instances where the names are identical it is probable that the Hopi designation has been derived from the Hano rather than vice versa, and in those cases where the Hano people know a katcina by its Hopi name it is possible that their knowledge of it came from their neighbors rather than from their old home on the Rio Grande.

The substitution of a Tanoan name for a Hopi katcina for its original name often sheds light on the character of the original. Thus Muyiñ wüqtaka is the Tanoan Nañoikusi, Earth Altar Man; Nañoiu-

---

[a] See The Winter Solstice Ceremony at Walpi, American Anthropologist, vol. XI, 1898, p. 65, 101.
[b] Called Kwatoku, Eagle-sky-one, High-sky-eagle; one of the sun birds.

PLATE LX

AHÜLANI

PLATE LXI

KOROCTÛ

PLATE LXII

PAKIOKWIK   KE TOWA BISENA   TURTUMSI

PLATE LXIII

OWA

CAKWAHONAU

TOHO

kwia, Earth Altar Woman, is called in Hopi Tuwapoñtumsi. The
lists follow:

Hopi name	Hano (Tanoan) name
Alosaka	Ceni
Añya	Oñkweñi
Atocle	Atocle
Caiastacana	Katcinetcen
Calako	Calako
Cipikne	Orlakepenne
Citoto	Porpinki
Citulilü	Citulilü
Coho	Agaiyo
Cotokinuñwû	Kwentulaci
Eototo	Tcemulo
Hahai wüqti	Pokikwia
Hakto	Parsepenne
Helilülü	Helilülü
Hokyaña	Koñtedje
Hototo	Sempotañle
Humis	Tsewe
Kaisale	Teñtaiye
Kalektaka (Akus)	Potaiye
Kawikoli	Papepekanne
Kiwatoka	Tcete
Kokle	Kokle
Kokopelli	Nipokwaiye
Kokyan wüqti	Yowanosaiye
Koroctû	Estoroka
Kwacus Alektaka	Zekwañsaiye
Kwahu	Tce
Macmahola	Peñemo
Masauû	Pene
Monwû	Mahone
Muyiñwû mana	Nañoiukwia
Muyiñwû taka	Nañoikusi
Nakiatcop	Pelekayi
Natacka	Natacka
Nüvak	Poñ
Pakwabi	Yütce
Palülükoñ	Avaiyo
Paluña hoya	Towatokwena
Patcosk	Kweñtcelepoe
Pautiwa	Pautiwa

Hopi name	Hano (Tanoan) name
Pawik	Orpin
Püükoñ hoya	Ewaile
Sio	Tconi
Sio Avatc hoya	Potedji
Sowiñwû	Peñ
Soyohim	Temedje
Soyoko	Soyoko
Sumaikoli	Sumaikoli
Talatumsi	Cenikwia
Tataukyamû	Tcipiwaiye
Tatcükti	Uñtamellipo
Tcabaiyo	Tcabaiyo
Tcakwaina	Tcakwaina
Tcilikomato	Kwandepe
Tcolawitze	Tcolawitze
Tcüb	Ton
Tehabe	Hoho-Pocililü
Telavai	Zuñtele
Tiwenu	Tiwenu
Tumae	Oñtcen
Tuñwup	Ho
Türkwinû	Pompin
Wakac	Wakac
Wukokot	Tekwede
Wupamau	Tceta
Wüwüyomo	Senna
Yehoho	Chikokakyan
Yohozro wüqti	Imbesaiye

ORIGIN OF FOREIGN KATCINAS

A few facts have been gathered regarding the legendary derivation
or origin of certain katcinas. The names of these katcinas are given
below, with the clans which are reputed to have brought them to Walpi
or other Hopi pueblos of the East mesa, and the pueblos from which
they are supposed to have come. Several of these are now in ruins.

Pakatcomo (Patki clan) [a]

Lakone mana	Soyal mana
Cotokinuñwû	Hopi Calako mana
Palülükoñ	Türkwinû [b]
Ahülani (Soyal katcina)	Türkwinû mana

[a] Pakatcomo is the name of a ruin in the Walpi valley, where the Patki and related clans lived
after they abandoned Homolobi and other pueblos farther south, as already stated.

[b] The name refers to San Francisco mountains. It is therefore doubtful whether this katcina came
from Pakatcomo.

Kicyuba (Katcina clan) [a]

Wüwükoti	Tcüelawû [b]
Ahül	Hele
Anwücnaco taka	Wupamau
Tuñwup	Aña
Tuñwup taadta	

Awatobi (Pakab clan) [c]

Tcanaû	Mamzrau mana
Püükoñ	Palahiko mana
Paluña hoya	Sowiñwû
Owakül tiyo	Soyok taka
Owakül mana	Soyok mana
Alosaka	Kwewû

Sikyatki (Kokop clan)

Masauû	Hemico
Eototo	Hopiñyû
Nakopan hoya	

Tuwanacabi (Honani clan) [d]

Wüwüyomo	Buli mana

Zuñi

By far the largest number of katcinas in Walpi and Sichumovi were derived from Zuñi, and these generally preserve their Zuñi names:

Sio Humis	Tcolawitze
Sio Humis taadta	Atocle
Sio Avatc hoya	Kwacus Alek taka
Hopak katcina	Alo mana
Hopak mana	Caiastacana
Kaisale and mana	Hototo
Citulilü	Powa
Sio Calako	Kaisale
Pawik	Sumaikoli
Soyowa	Tcakwaina
Teük	Tcakwaina mana
Kawikoli	Tcakwaina taadta
Malo	Tcakwaina yuadta
Sio	Loiica
Helilülü	Kokopelli
Sio mana	Kokopelli mana
Hokyaña	Tcosbuci
Pautiwa	Soyan ep
Ciwikoli	Samo wüqtaka

---

[a] Kicyuba, a very sacred place to the Katcina clan, and the site ot their former home. Water from Kicyuba is regarded as very potent in ceremonies for rain.

[b] A mountain not far from Kicyuba is called Tcüelawû's Chair.

[c] Awatobi is a historic ruin destroyed the last year of the seventeenth century by warriors from the other Hopi pueblos. See Seventeenth Annual Report of the Bureau of American Ethnology, 1898.

[d] A ruin not far from Oraibi, where it is said the katcinas emerged from the under world and gave the katcina mysteries to the Honani clan.

Hano

The following katcinas are distinctively Tanoan, and were derived from the pueblo of Hano:

Wakac	Yohozro wüqti
Nalucala	Mucaias taka
Ke Towa Bisena	Macaias mana
Nüvak	

Several katcinas personated by the Hopis are called by Navaho names and are said to have been derived from the tribe, the name of which they sometimes have:

Tenebidji	Owa katcina taka
Naactadji	Owa katcina mana
Yebitcai *a*	

ALPHABET USED IN SPELLING NAMES

The vowels a, e, i, o, u have their continental values, as in father, they, pique, go, true. E, i, and u are broadened when used with a breve (ĕ, ĭ, ŭ) or before a doubled consonant, assuming their values in met, hit, and put. Û is pronounced as u in but, au as ow in cow, ai as in aisle; ü varies from German ö to ü, French eu to u.

The consonants p, b, t, d, k, f, v, s, z, l, m, n, w, y, h have approximately their English values, but p, b, f, and v, and t and d are difficult to distinguish. C is pronounced as in ocean (as sh in shed), j as z in azure (French j), tc as ch in chew, dj as j in jaw, g as in get, ñ as ng in sing, q as German ch in ich; r is obscure, never rolled.

---

a The Hopi translate this Navaho name Katcina kwamû, Grandfather of the katcinas.

INDEX

A CATALOG OF SELECTED
DOVER BOOKS
IN ALL FIELDS OF INTEREST

A CATALOG OF SELECTED DOVER
BOOKS IN ALL FIELDS OF INTEREST

DRAWINGS OF REMBRANDT, edited by Seymour Slive. Updated Lippmann, Hofstede de Groot edition, with definitive scholarly apparatus. All portraits, biblical sketches, landscapes, nudes. Oriental figures, classical studies, together with selection of work by followers. 550 illustrations. Total of 630pp. 9⅛ × 12¼.
21485-0, 21486-9 Pa., Two-vol. set $25.00

GHOST AND HORROR STORIES OF AMBROSE BIERCE, Ambrose Bierce. 24 tales vividly imagined, strangely prophetic, and decades ahead of their time in technical skill: "The Damned Thing," "An Inhabitant of Carcosa," "The Eyes of the Panther," "Moxon's Master," and 20 more. 199pp. 5⅜ × 8½. 20767-6 Pa. $3.95

ETHICAL WRITINGS OF MAIMONIDES, Maimonides. Most significant ethical works of great medieval sage, newly translated for utmost precision, readability. Laws Concerning Character Traits, Eight Chapters, more. 192pp. 5⅜ × 8½.
24522-5 Pa. $4.50

THE EXPLORATION OF THE COLORADO RIVER AND ITS CANYONS, J. W. Powell. Full text of Powell's 1,000-mile expedition down the fabled Colorado in 1869. Superb account of terrain, geology, vegetation, Indians, famine, mutiny, treacherous rapids, mighty canyons, during exploration of last unknown part of continental U.S. 400pp. 5⅜ × 8½. 20094-9 Pa. $6.95

HISTORY OF PHILOSOPHY, Julián Marías. Clearest one-volume history on the market. Every major philosopher and dozens of others, to Existentialism and later. 505pp. 5⅜ × 8½. 21739-6 Pa. $8.50

ALL ABOUT LIGHTNING, Martin A. Uman. Highly readable non-technical survey of nature and causes of lightning, thunderstorms, ball lightning, St. Elmo's Fire, much more. Illustrated. 192pp. 5⅜ × 8½. 25237-X Pa. $5.95

SAILING ALONE AROUND THE WORLD, Captain Joshua Slocum. First man to sail around the world, alone, in small boat. One of great feats of seamanship told in delightful manner. 67 illustrations. 294pp. 5⅜ × 8½. 20326-3 Pa. $4.50

LETTERS AND NOTES ON THE MANNERS, CUSTOMS AND CONDITIONS OF THE NORTH AMERICAN INDIANS, George Catlin. Classic account of life among Plains Indians: ceremonies, hunt, warfare, etc. 312 plates. 572pp. of text. 6⅛ × 9¼. 22118-0, 22119-9 Pa. Two-vol. set $15.90

ALASKA: The Harriman Expedition, 1899, John Burroughs, John Muir, et al. Informative, engrossing accounts of two-month, 9,000-mile expedition. Native peoples, wildlife, forests, geography, salmon industry, glaciers, more. Profusely illustrated. 240 black-and-white line drawings. 124 black-and-white photographs. 3 maps. Index. 576pp. 5⅜ × 8½. 25109-8 Pa. $11.95

THE BOOK OF BEASTS: Being a Translation from a Latin Bestiary of the Twelfth Century, T. H. White. Wonderful catalog real and fanciful beasts: manticore, griffin, phoenix, amphivius, jaculus, many more. White's witty erudite commentary on scientific, historical aspects. Fascinating glimpse of medieval mind. Illustrated. 296pp. 5⅜ × 8¼. (Available in U.S. only)   24609-4 Pa. $5.95

FRANK LLOYD WRIGHT: ARCHITECTURE AND NATURE With 160 Illustrations, Donald Hoffmann. Profusely illustrated study of influence of nature—especially prairie—on Wright's designs for Fallingwater, Robie House, Guggenheim Museum, other masterpieces. 96pp. 9¼ × 10¾.   25098-9 Pa. $7.95

FRANK LLOYD WRIGHT'S FALLINGWATER, Donald Hoffmann. Wright's famous waterfall house: planning and construction of organic idea. History of site, owners, Wright's personal involvement. Photographs of various stages of building. Preface by Edgar Kaufmann, Jr. 100 illustrations. 112pp. 9¼ × 10.
23671-4 Pa. $7.95

YEARS WITH FRANK LLOYD WRIGHT: Apprentice to Genius, Edgar Tafel. Insightful memoir by a former apprentice presents a revealing portrait of Wright the man, the inspired teacher, the greatest American architect. 372 black-and-white illustrations. Preface. Index. vi + 228pp. 8¼ × 11.   24801-1 Pa. $9.95

THE STORY OF KING ARTHUR AND HIS KNIGHTS, Howard Pyle. Enchanting version of King Arthur fable has delighted generations with imaginative narratives of exciting adventures and unforgettable illustrations by the author. 41 illustrations. xviii + 313pp. 6⅛ × 9¼.   21445-1 Pa. $5.95

THE GODS OF THE EGYPTIANS, E. A. Wallis Budge. Thorough coverage of numerous gods of ancient Egypt by foremost Egyptologist. Information on evolution of cults, rites and gods; the cult of Osiris; the Book of the Dead and its rites; the sacred animals and birds; Heaven and Hell; and more. 956pp. 6⅛ × 9¼.
22055-9, 22056-7 Pa., Two-vol. set $20.00

A THEOLOGICO-POLITICAL TREATISE, Benedict Spinoza. Also contains unfinished *Political Treatise*. Great classic on religious liberty, theory of government on common consent. R. Elwes translation. Total of 421pp. 5⅜ × 8½.
20249-6 Pa. $6.95

INCIDENTS OF TRAVEL IN CENTRAL AMERICA, CHIAPAS, AND YUCATAN, John L. Stephens. Almost single-handed discovery of Maya culture; exploration of ruined cities, monuments, temples; customs of Indians. 115 drawings. 892pp. 5⅜ × 8½.   22404-X, 22405-8 Pa., Two-vol. set $15.90

LOS CAPRICHOS, Francisco Goya. 80 plates of wild, grotesque monsters and caricatures. Prado manuscript included. 183pp. 6⅜ × 9⅜.   22384-1 Pa. $4.95

AUTOBIOGRAPHY: The Story of My Experiments with Truth, Mohandas K. Gandhi. Not hagiography, but Gandhi in his own words. Boyhood, legal studies, purification, the growth of the Satyagraha (nonviolent protest) movement. Critical, inspiring work of the man who freed India. 480pp. 5⅜ × 8½. (Available in U.S. only)
24593-4 Pa. $6.95

ILLUSTRATED DICTIONARY OF HISTORIC ARCHITECTURE, edited by Cyril M. Harris. Extraordinary compendium of clear, concise definitions for over 5,000 important architectural terms complemented by over 2,000 line drawings. Covers full spectrum of architecture from ancient ruins to 20th-century Modernism. Preface. 592pp. 7½ × 9⅜. 24444-X Pa. $14.95

THE NIGHT BEFORE CHRISTMAS, Clement Moore. Full text, and woodcuts from original 1848 book. Also critical, historical material. 19 illustrations. 40pp. 4⅝ × 6. 22797-9 Pa. $2.25

THE LESSON OF JAPANESE ARCHITECTURE: 165 Photographs, Jiro Harada. Memorable gallery of 165 photographs taken in the 1930's of exquisite Japanese homes of the well-to-do and historic buildings. 13 line diagrams. 192pp. 8⅜ × 11¼. 24778-3 Pa. $8.95

THE AUTOBIOGRAPHY OF CHARLES DARWIN AND SELECTED LETTERS, edited by Francis Darwin. The fascinating life of eccentric genius composed of an intimate memoir by Darwin (intended for his children); commentary by his son, Francis; hundreds of fragments from notebooks, journals, papers; and letters to and from Lyell, Hooker, Huxley, Wallace and Henslow. xi + 365pp. 5⅜ × 8. 20479-0 Pa. $5.95

WONDERS OF THE SKY: Observing Rainbows, Comets, Eclipses, the Stars and Other Phenomena, Fred Schaaf. Charming, easy-to-read poetic guide to all manner of celestial events visible to the naked eye. Mock suns, glories, Belt of Venus, more. Illustrated. 299pp. 5¼ × 8¼. 24402-4 Pa. $7.95

BURNHAM'S CELESTIAL HANDBOOK, Robert Burnham, Jr. Thorough guide to the stars beyond our solar system. Exhaustive treatment. Alphabetical by constellation: Andromeda to Cetus in Vol. 1; Chamaeleon to Orion in Vol. 2; and Pavo to Vulpecula in Vol. 3. Hundreds of illustrations. Index in Vol. 3. 2,000pp. 6⅛ × 9¼. 23567-X, 23568-8, 23673-0 Pa., Three-vol. set $36.85

STAR NAMES: Their Lore and Meaning, Richard Hinckley Allen. Fascinating history of names various cultures have given to constellations and literary and folkloristic uses that have been made of stars. Indexes to subjects. Arabic and Greek names. Biblical references. Bibliography. 563pp. 5⅜ × 8½. 21079-0 Pa. $7.95

THIRTY YEARS THAT SHOOK PHYSICS: The Story of Quantum Theory, George Gamow. Lucid, accessible introduction to influential theory of energy and matter. Careful explanations of Dirac's anti-particles, Bohr's model of the atom, much more. 12 plates. Numerous drawings. 240pp. 5⅜ × 8½. 24895-X Pa. $4.95

CHINESE DOMESTIC FURNITURE IN PHOTOGRAPHS AND MEASURED DRAWINGS, Gustav Ecke. A rare volume, now affordably priced for antique collectors, furniture buffs and art historians. Detailed review of styles ranging from early Shang to late Ming. Unabridged republication. 161 black-and-white drawings, photos. Total of 224pp. 8⅜ × 11¼. (Available in U.S. only) 25171-3 Pa. $12.95

VINCENT VAN GOGH: A Biography, Julius Meier-Graefe. Dynamic, penetrating study of artist's life, relationship with brother, Theo, painting techniques, travels, more. Readable, engrossing. 160pp. 5⅜ × 8½. (Available in U.S. only) 25253-1 Pa. $3.95

SUNDIALS, Albert Waugh. Far and away the best, most thorough coverage of ideas, mathematics concerned, types, construction, adjusting anywhere. Over 100 illustrations. 230pp. 5⅜ × 8½. 22947-5 Pa. $4.00

PICTURE HISTORY OF THE NORMANDIE: With 190 Illustrations, Frank O. Braynard. Full story of legendary French ocean liner: Art Deco interiors, design innovations, furnishings, celebrities, maiden voyage, tragic fire, much more. Extensive text. 144pp. 8⅜ × 11¾. 25257-4 Pa. $9.95

THE FIRST AMERICAN COOKBOOK: A Facsimile of "American Cookery," 1796, Amelia Simmons. Facsimile of the first American-written cookbook published in the United States contains authentic recipes for colonial favorites—pumpkin pudding, winter squash pudding, spruce beer, Indian slapjacks, and more. Introductory Essay and Glossary of colonial cooking terms. 80pp. 5⅜ × 8½. 24710-4 Pa. $3.50

101 PUZZLES IN THOUGHT AND LOGIC, C. R. Wylie, Jr. Solve murders and robberies, find out which fishermen are liars, how a blind man could possibly identify a color—purely by your own reasoning! 107pp. 5⅜ × 8½. 20367-0 Pa. $2.00

THE BOOK OF WORLD-FAMOUS MUSIC—CLASSICAL, POPULAR AND FOLK, James J. Fuld. Revised and enlarged republication of landmark work in musico-bibliography. Full information about nearly 1,000 songs and compositions including first lines of music and lyrics. New supplement. Index. 800pp. 5⅜ × 8¼. 24857-7 Pa. $14.95

ANTHROPOLOGY AND MODERN LIFE, Franz Boas. Great anthropologist's classic treatise on race and culture. Introduction by Ruth Bunzel. Only inexpensive paperback edition. 255pp. 5⅜ × 8½. 25245-0 Pa. $5.95

THE TALE OF PETER RABBIT, Beatrix Potter. The inimitable Peter's terrifying adventure in Mr. McGregor's garden, with all 27 wonderful, full-color Potter illustrations. 55pp. 4¼ × 5½. (Available in U.S. only) 22827-4 Pa. $1.75

THREE PROPHETIC SCIENCE FICTION NOVELS, H. G. Wells. *When the Sleeper Wakes, A Story of the Days to Come* and *The Time Machine* (full version). 335pp. 5⅜ × 8½. (Available in U.S. only) 20605-X Pa. $5.95

APICIUS COOKERY AND DINING IN IMPERIAL ROME, edited and translated by Joseph Dommers Vehling. Oldest known cookbook in existence offers readers a clear picture of what foods Romans ate, how they prepared them, etc. 49 illustrations. 301pp. 6⅛ × 9¼. 23563-7 Pa. $6.00

SHAKESPEARE LEXICON AND QUOTATION DICTIONARY, Alexander Schmidt. Full definitions, locations, shades of meaning of every word in plays and poems. More than 50,000 exact quotations. 1,485pp. 6½ × 9¼. 22726-X, 22727-8 Pa., Two-vol. set $27.90

THE WORLD'S GREAT SPEECHES, edited by Lewis Copeland and Lawrence W. Lamm. Vast collection of 278 speeches from Greeks to 1970. Powerful and effective models; unique look at history. 842pp. 5⅜ × 8½. 20468-5 Pa. $10.95

ILLUSTRATED GUIDE TO SHAKER FURNITURE, Robert Meader. All furniture and appurtenances, with much on unknown local styles. 235 photos. 146pp. 9 × 12. 22819-3 Pa. $7.95

WHALE SHIPS AND WHALING: A Pictorial Survey, George Francis Dow. Over 200 vintage engravings, drawings, photographs of barks, brigs, cutters, other vessels. Also harpoons, lances, whaling guns, many other artifacts. Comprehensive text by foremost authority. 207 black-and-white illustrations. 288pp. 6 × 9. 24808-9 Pa. $8.95

THE BERTRAMS, Anthony Trollope. Powerful portrayal of blind self-will and thwarted ambition includes one of Trollope's most heartrending love stories. 497pp. 5⅜ × 8½. 25119-5 Pa. $8.95

ADVENTURES WITH A HAND LENS, Richard Headstrom. Clearly written guide to observing and studying flowers and grasses, fish scales, moth and insect wings, egg cases, buds, feathers, seeds, leaf scars, moss, molds, ferns, common crystals, etc.—all with an ordinary, inexpensive magnifying glass. 209 exact line drawings aid in your discoveries. 220pp. 5⅜ × 8½. 23330-8 Pa. $3.95

RODIN ON ART AND ARTISTS, Auguste Rodin. Great sculptor's candid, wide-ranging comments on meaning of art; great artists; relation of sculpture to poetry, painting, music; philosophy of life, more. 76 superb black-and-white illustrations of Rodin's sculpture, drawings and prints. 119pp. 8⅜ × 11¼. 24487-3 Pa. $6.95

FIFTY CLASSIC FRENCH FILMS, 1912–1982: A Pictorial Record, Anthony Slide. Memorable stills from Grand Illusion, Beauty and the Beast, Hiroshima, Mon Amour, many more. Credits, plot synopses, reviews, etc. 160pp. 8¼ × 11. 25256-6 Pa. $11.95

THE PRINCIPLES OF PSYCHOLOGY, William James. Famous long course complete, unabridged. Stream of thought, time perception, memory, experimental methods; great work decades ahead of its time. 94 figures. 1,391pp. 5⅜ × 8½. 20381-6, 20382-4 Pa., Two-vol. set $19.90

BODIES IN A BOOKSHOP, R. T. Campbell. Challenging mystery of blackmail and murder with ingenious plot and superbly drawn characters. In the best tradition of British suspense fiction. 192pp. 5⅜ × 8½. 24720-1 Pa. $3.95

CALLAS: PORTRAIT OF A PRIMA DONNA, George Jellinek. Renowned commentator on the musical scene chronicles incredible career and life of the most controversial, fascinating, influential operatic personality of our time. 64 black-and-white photographs. 416pp. 5⅜ × 8¼. 25047-4 Pa. $7.95

GEOMETRY, RELATIVITY AND THE FOURTH DIMENSION, Rudolph Rucker. Exposition of fourth dimension, concepts of relativity as Flatland characters continue adventures. Popular, easily followed yet accurate, profound. 141 illustrations. 133pp. 5⅜ × 8½. 23400-2 Pa. $3.50

HOUSEHOLD STORIES BY THE BROTHERS GRIMM, with pictures by Walter Crane. 53 classic stories—Rumpelstiltskin, Rapunzel, Hansel and Gretel, the Fisherman and his Wife, Snow White, Tom Thumb, Sleeping Beauty, Cinderella, and so much more—lavishly illustrated with original 19th century drawings. 114 illustrations. x + 269pp. 5⅜ × 8½. 21080-4 Pa. $4.50

HOW TO WRITE, Gertrude Stein. Gertrude Stein claimed anyone could understand her unconventional writing—here are clues to help. Fascinating improvisations, language experiments, explanations illuminate Stein's craft and the art of writing. Total of 414pp. 4⅜ × 6⅜. 23144-5 Pa. $5.95

ADVENTURES AT SEA IN THE GREAT AGE OF SAIL: Five Firsthand Narratives, edited by Elliot Snow. Rare true accounts of exploration, whaling, shipwreck, fierce natives, trade, shipboard life, more. 33 illustrations. Introduction. 353pp. 5⅜ × 8½. 25177-2 Pa. $7.95

THE HERBAL OR GENERAL HISTORY OF PLANTS, John Gerard. Classic descriptions of about 2,850 plants—with over 2,700 illustrations—includes Latin and English names, physical descriptions, varieties, time and place of growth, more. 2,706 illustrations. xlv + 1,678pp. 8½ × 12¼. 23147-X Cloth. $75.00

DOROTHY AND THE WIZARD IN OZ, L. Frank Baum. Dorothy and the Wizard visit the center of the Earth, where people are vegetables, glass houses grow and Oz characters reappear. Classic sequel to *Wizard of Oz*. 256pp. 5⅜ × 8. 24714-7 Pa. $4.95

SONGS OF EXPERIENCE: Facsimile Reproduction with 26 Plates in Full Color, William Blake. This facsimile of Blake's original "Illuminated Book" reproduces 26 full-color plates from a rare 1826 edition. Includes "The Tyger," "London," "Holy Thursday," and other immortal poems. 26 color plates. Printed text of poems. 48pp. 5¼ × 7. 24636-1 Pa. $3.50

SONGS OF INNOCENCE, William Blake. The first and most popular of Blake's famous "Illuminated Books," in a facsimile edition reproducing all 31 brightly colored plates. Additional printed text of each poem. 64pp. 5¼ × 7. 22764-2 Pa. $3.50

PRECIOUS STONES, Max Bauer. Classic, thorough study of diamonds, rubies, emeralds, garnets, etc.: physical character, occurrence, properties, use, similar topics. 20 plates, 8 in color. 94 figures. 659pp. 6⅛ × 9¼. 21910-0, 21911-9 Pa., Two-vol. set $14.90

ENCYCLOPEDIA OF VICTORIAN NEEDLEWORK, S. F. A. Caulfeild and Blanche Saward. Full, precise descriptions of stitches, techniques for dozens of needlecrafts—most exhaustive reference of its kind. Over 800 figures. Total of 679pp. 8⅛ × 11. Two volumes. Vol. 1 22800-2 Pa. $10.95
Vol. 2 22801-0 Pa. $10.95

THE MARVELOUS LAND OF OZ, L. Frank Baum. Second Oz book, the Scarecrow and Tin Woodman are back with hero named Tip, Oz magic. 136 illustrations. 287pp. 5⅜ × 8½. 20692-0 Pa. $5.95

WILD FOWL DECOYS, Joel Barber. Basic book on the subject, by foremost authority and collector. Reveals history of decoy making and rigging, place in American culture, different kinds of decoys, how to make them, and how to use them. 140 plates. 156pp. 7⅞ × 10¾. 20011-6 Pa. $7.95

HISTORY OF LACE, Mrs. Bury Palliser. Definitive, profusely illustrated chronicle of lace from earliest times to late 19th century. Laces of Italy, Greece, England, France, Belgium, etc. Landmark of needlework scholarship. 266 illustrations. 672pp. 6⅛ × 9¼. 24742-2 Pa. $14.95

THE BLUE FAIRY BOOK, Andrew Lang. The first, most famous collection, with many familiar tales: Little Red Riding Hood, Aladdin and the Wonderful Lamp, Puss in Boots, Sleeping Beauty, Hansel and Gretel, Rumpelstiltskin; 37 in all. 138 illustrations. 390pp. 5⅜ × 8½. 21437-0 Pa. $5.95

THE STORY OF THE CHAMPIONS OF THE ROUND TABLE, Howard Pyle. Sir Launcelot, Sir Tristram and Sir Percival in spirited adventures of love and triumph retold in Pyle's inimitable style. 50 drawings, 31 full-page. xviii + 329pp. 6½ × 9¼. 21883-X Pa. $6.95

AUDUBON AND HIS JOURNALS, Maria Audubon. Unmatched two-volume portrait of the great artist, naturalist and author contains his journals, an excellent biography by his granddaughter, expert annotations by the noted ornithologist, Dr. Elliott Coues, and 37 superb illustrations. Total of 1,200pp. 5⅜ × 8.
Vol. I 25143-8 Pa. $8.95
Vol. II 25144-6 Pa. $8.95

GREAT DINOSAUR HUNTERS AND THEIR DISCOVERIES, Edwin H. Colbert. Fascinating, lavishly illustrated chronicle of dinosaur research, 1820's to 1960. Achievements of Cope, Marsh, Brown, Buckland, Mantell, Huxley, many others. 384pp. 5¼ × 8¼. 24701-5 Pa. $6.95

THE TASTEMAKERS, Russell Lynes. Informal, illustrated social history of American taste 1850's–1950's. First popularized categories Highbrow, Lowbrow, Middlebrow. 129 illustrations. New (1979) afterword. 384pp. 6 × 9.
23993-4 Pa. $6.95

DOUBLE CROSS PURPOSES, Ronald A. Knox. A treasure hunt in the Scottish Highlands, an old map, unidentified corpse, surprise discoveries keep reader guessing in this cleverly intricate tale of financial skullduggery. 2 black-and-white maps. 320pp. 5⅜ × 8½. (Available in U.S. only) 25032-6 Pa. $5.95

AUTHENTIC VICTORIAN DECORATION AND ORNAMENTATION IN FULL COLOR: 46 Plates from "Studies in Design," Christopher Dresser. Superb full-color lithographs reproduced from rare original portfolio of a major Victorian designer. 48pp. 9¼ × 12¼. 25083-0 Pa. $7.95

PRIMITIVE ART, Franz Boas. Remains the best text ever prepared on subject, thoroughly discussing Indian, African, Asian, Australian, and, especially, Northern American primitive art. Over 950 illustrations show ceramics, masks, totem poles, weapons, textiles, paintings, much more. 376pp. 5⅜ × 8. 20025-6 Pa. $6.95

SIDELIGHTS ON RELATIVITY, Albert Einstein. Unabridged republication of two lectures delivered by the great physicist in 1920–21. *Ether and Relativity* and *Geometry and Experience*. Elegant ideas in non-mathematical form, accessible to intelligent layman. vi + 56pp. 5⅜ × 8½. 24511-X Pa. $2.95

THE WIT AND HUMOR OF OSCAR WILDE, edited by Alvin Redman. More than 1,000 ripostes, paradoxes, wisecracks: Work is the curse of the drinking classes, I can resist everything except temptation, etc. 258pp. 5⅜ × 8½. 20602-5 Pa. $3.95

ADVENTURES WITH A MICROSCOPE, Richard Headstrom. 59 adventures with clothing fibers, protozoa, ferns and lichens, roots and leaves, much more. 142 illustrations. 232pp. 5⅜ × 8½. 23471-1 Pa. $3.95

PLANTS OF THE BIBLE, Harold N. Moldenke and Alma L. Moldenke. Standard reference to all 230 plants mentioned in Scriptures. Latin name, biblical reference, uses, modern identity, much more. Unsurpassed encyclopedic resource for scholars, botanists, nature lovers, students of Bible. Bibliography. Indexes. 123 black-and-white illustrations. 384pp. 6 × 9. 25069-5 Pa. $8.95

FAMOUS AMERICAN WOMEN: A Biographical Dictionary from Colonial Times to the Present, Robert McHenry, ed. From Pocahontas to Rosa Parks, 1,035 distinguished American women documented in separate biographical entries. Accurate, up-to-date data, numerous categories, spans 400 years. Indices. 493pp. 6½ × 9¼. 24523-3 Pa. $9.95

THE FABULOUS INTERIORS OF THE GREAT OCEAN LINERS IN HISTORIC PHOTOGRAPHS, William H. Miller, Jr. Some 200 superb photographs capture exquisite interiors of world's great "floating palaces"—1890's to 1980's: *Titanic, Ile de France, Queen Elizabeth, United States, Europa,* more. Approx. 200 black-and-white photographs. Captions. Text. Introduction. 160pp. 8⅞ × 11¾. 24756-2 Pa. $9.95

THE GREAT LUXURY LINERS, 1927–1954: A Photographic Record, William H. Miller, Jr. Nostalgic tribute to heyday of ocean liners. 186 photos of Ile de France, Normandie, Leviathan, Queen Elizabeth, United States, many others. Interior and exterior views. Introduction. Captions. 160pp. 9 × 12. 24056-8 Pa. $9.95

A NATURAL HISTORY OF THE DUCKS, John Charles Phillips. Great landmark of ornithology offers complete detailed coverage of nearly 200 species and subspecies of ducks: gadwall, sheldrake, merganser, pintail, many more. 74 full-color plates, 102 black-and-white. Bibliography. Total of 1,920pp. 8⅝ × 11¼. 25141-1, 25142-X Cloth. Two-vol. set $100.00

THE SEAWEED HANDBOOK: An Illustrated Guide to Seaweeds from North Carolina to Canada, Thomas F. Lee. Concise reference covers 78 species. Scientific and common names, habitat, distribution, more. Finding keys for easy identification. 224pp. 5⅜ × 8½. 25215-9 Pa. $5.95

THE TEN BOOKS OF ARCHITECTURE: The 1755 Leoni Edition, Leon Battista Alberti. Rare classic helped introduce the glories of ancient architecture to the Renaissance. 68 black-and-white plates. 336pp. 8⅜ × 11¼. 25239-6 Pa. $14.95

MISS MACKENZIE, Anthony Trollope. Minor masterpieces by Victorian master unmasks many truths about life in 19th-century England. First inexpensive edition in years. 392pp. 5⅜ × 8½. 25201-9 Pa. $7.95

THE RIME OF THE ANCIENT MARINER, Gustave Doré, Samuel Taylor Coleridge. Dramatic engravings considered by many to be his greatest work. The terrifying space of the open sea, the storms and whirlpools of an unknown ocean, the ice of Antarctica, more—all rendered in a powerful, chilling manner. Full text. 38 plates. 77pp. 9¼ × 12. 22305-1 Pa. $4.95

THE EXPEDITIONS OF ZEBULON MONTGOMERY PIKE, Zebulon Montgomery Pike. Fascinating first-hand accounts (1805–6) of exploration of Mississippi River, Indian wars, capture by Spanish dragoons, much more. 1,088pp. 5⅜ × 8½. 25254-X, 25255-8 Pa. Two-vol. set $23.90

A CONCISE HISTORY OF PHOTOGRAPHY: Third Revised Edition, Helmut Gernsheim. Best one-volume history—camera obscura, photochemistry, daguerreotypes, evolution of cameras, film, more. Also artistic aspects—landscape, portraits, fine art, etc. 281 black-and-white photographs. 26 in color. 176pp. 8⅜ × 11¼. 25128-4 Pa. $12.95

THE DORÉ BIBLE ILLUSTRATIONS, Gustave Doré. 241 detailed plates from the Bible: the Creation scenes, Adam and Eve, Flood, Babylon, battle sequences, life of Jesus, etc. Each plate is accompanied by the verses from the King James version of the Bible. 241pp. 9 × 12. 23004-X Pa. $8.95

HUGGER-MUGGER IN THE LOUVRE, Elliot Paul. Second Homer Evans mystery-comedy. Theft at the Louvre involves sleuth in hilarious, madcap caper. "A knockout."—Books. 336pp. 5⅜ × 8½. 25185-3 Pa. $5.95

FLATLAND, E. A. Abbott. Intriguing and enormously popular science-fiction classic explores the complexities of trying to survive as a two-dimensional being in a three-dimensional world. Amusingly illustrated by the author. 16 illustrations. 103pp. 5⅜ × 8½. 20001-9 Pa. $2.00

THE HISTORY OF THE LEWIS AND CLARK EXPEDITION, Meriwether Lewis and William Clark, edited by Elliott Coues. Classic edition of Lewis and Clark's day-by-day journals that later became the basis for U.S. claims to Oregon and the West. Accurate and invaluable geographical, botanical, biological, meteorological and anthropological material. Total of 1,508pp. 5⅜ × 8½.
21268-8, 21269-6, 21270-X Pa. Three-vol. set $25.50

LANGUAGE, TRUTH AND LOGIC, Alfred J. Ayer. Famous, clear introduction to Vienna, Cambridge schools of Logical Positivism. Role of philosophy, elimination of metaphysics, nature of analysis, etc. 160pp. 5⅜ × 8½. (Available in U.S. and Canada only) 20010-8 Pa. $2.95

MATHEMATICS FOR THE NONMATHEMATICIAN, Morris Kline. Detailed, college-level treatment of mathematics in cultural and historical context, with numerous exercises. For liberal arts students. Preface. Recommended Reading Lists. Tables. Index. Numerous black-and-white figures. xvi + 641pp. 5⅜ × 8½.
24823-2 Pa. $11.95

28 SCIENCE FICTION STORIES, H. G. Wells. Novels, *Star Begotten* and *Men Like Gods,* plus 26 short stories: "Empire of the Ants," "A Story of the Stone Age," "The Stolen Bacillus," "In the Abyss," etc. 915pp. 5⅜ × 8½. (Available in U.S. only)
20265-8 Cloth. $10.95

HANDBOOK OF PICTORIAL SYMBOLS, Rudolph Modley. 3,250 signs and symbols, many systems in full; official or heavy commercial use. Arranged by subject. Most in Pictorial Archive series. 143pp. 8⅛ × 11. 23357-X Pa. $5.95

INCIDENTS OF TRAVEL IN YUCATAN, John L. Stephens. Classic (1843) exploration of jungles of Yucatan, looking for evidences of Maya civilization. Travel adventures, Mexican and Indian culture, etc. Total of 669pp. 5⅜ × 8½.
20926-1, 20927-X Pa., Two-vol. set $9.90

DEGAS: An Intimate Portrait, Ambroise Vollard. Charming, anecdotal memoir by famous art dealer of one of the greatest 19th-century French painters. 14 black-and-white illustrations. Introduction by Harold L. Van Doren. 96pp. 5⅜ × 8½.
25131-4 Pa. $3.95

PERSONAL NARRATIVE OF A PILGRIMAGE TO ALMANDINAH AND MECCAH, Richard Burton. Great travel classic by remarkably colorful personality. Burton, disguised as a Moroccan, visited sacred shrines of Islam, narrowly escaping death. 47 illustrations. 959pp. 5⅜ × 8½. 21217-3, 21218-1 Pa., Two-vol. set $17.90

PHRASE AND WORD ORIGINS, A. H. Holt. Entertaining, reliable, modern study of more than 1,200 colorful words, phrases, origins and histories. Much unexpected information. 254pp. 5⅜ × 8½. 20758-7 Pa. $4.95

THE RED THUMB MARK, R. Austin Freeman. In this first Dr. Thorndyke case, the great scientific detective draws fascinating conclusions from the nature of a single fingerprint. Exciting story, authentic science. 320pp. 5⅜ × 8½. (Available in U.S. only) 25210-8 Pa. $5.95

AN EGYPTIAN HIEROGLYPHIC DICTIONARY, E. A. Wallis Budge. Monumental work containing about 25,000 words or terms that occur in texts ranging from 3000 B.C. to 600 A.D. Each entry consists of a transliteration of the word, the word in hieroglyphs, and the meaning in English. 1,314pp. 6⅜ × 10.
23615-3, 23616-1 Pa., Two-vol. set $27.90

THE COMPLEAT STRATEGYST: Being a Primer on the Theory of Games of Strategy, J. D. Williams. Highly entertaining classic describes, with many illustrated examples, how to select best strategies in conflict situations. Prefaces. Appendices. xvi + 268pp. 5⅜ × 8½. 25101-2 Pa. $5.95

THE ROAD TO OZ, L. Frank Baum. Dorothy meets the Shaggy Man, little Button-Bright and the Rainbow's beautiful daughter in this delightful trip to the magical Land of Oz. 272pp. 5⅜ × 8. 25208-6 Pa. $4.95

POINT AND LINE TO PLANE, Wassily Kandinsky. Seminal exposition of role of point, line, other elements in non-objective painting. Essential to understanding 20th-century art. 127 illustrations. 192pp. 6½ × 9¼. 23808-3 Pa. $4.50

LADY ANNA, Anthony Trollope. Moving chronicle of Countess Lovel's bitter struggle to win for herself and daughter Anna their rightful rank and fortune—perhaps at cost of sanity itself. 384pp. 5⅜ × 8½. 24669-8 Pa. $6.95

EGYPTIAN MAGIC, E. A. Wallis Budge. Sums up all that is known about magic in Ancient Egypt: the role of magic in controlling the gods, powerful amulets that warded off evil spirits, scarabs of immortality, use of wax images, formulas and spells, the secret name, much more. 253pp. 5⅜ × 8½. 22681-6 Pa. $4.00

THE DANCE OF SIVA, Ananda Coomaraswamy. Preeminent authority unfolds the vast metaphysic of India: the revelation of her art, conception of the universe, social organization, etc. 27 reproductions of art masterpieces. 192pp. 5⅜ × 8½.
24817-8 Pa. $5.95

CHRISTMAS CUSTOMS AND TRADITIONS, Clement A. Miles. Origin, evolution, significance of religious, secular practices. Caroling, gifts, yule logs, much more. Full, scholarly yet fascinating; non-sectarian. 400pp. 5⅜ × 8½.
23354-5 Pa. $6.50

THE HUMAN FIGURE IN MOTION, Eadweard Muybridge. More than 4,500 stopped-action photos, in action series, showing undraped men, women, children jumping, lying down, throwing, sitting, wrestling, carrying, etc. 390pp. 7⅞ × 10⅝.
20204-6 Cloth. $19.95

THE MAN WHO WAS THURSDAY, Gilbert Keith Chesterton. Witty, fast-paced novel about a club of anarchists in turn-of-the-century London. Brilliant social, religious, philosophical speculations. 128pp. 5⅜ × 8½.
25121-7 Pa. $3.95

A CEZANNE SKETCHBOOK: Figures, Portraits, Landscapes and Still Lifes, Paul Cezanne. Great artist experiments with tonal effects, light, mass, other qualities in over 100 drawings. A revealing view of developing master painter, precursor of Cubism. 102 black-and-white illustrations. 144pp. 8¾ × 6⅜.
24790-2 Pa. $5.95

AN ENCYCLOPEDIA OF BATTLES: Accounts of Over 1,560 Battles from 1479 B.C. to the Present, David Eggenberger. Presents essential details of every major battle in recorded history, from the first battle of Megiddo in 1479 B.C. to Grenada in 1984. List of Battle Maps. New Appendix covering the years 1967–1984. Index. 99 illustrations. 544pp. 6½ × 9¼.
24913-1 Pa. $14.95

AN ETYMOLOGICAL DICTIONARY OF MODERN ENGLISH, Ernest Weekley. Richest, fullest work, by foremost British lexicographer. Detailed word histories. Inexhaustible. Total of 856pp. 6½ × 9¼.
21873-2, 21874-0 Pa., Two-vol. set $17.00

WEBSTER'S AMERICAN MILITARY BIOGRAPHIES, edited by Robert McHenry. Over 1,000 figures who shaped 3 centuries of American military history. Detailed biographies of Nathan Hale, Douglas MacArthur, Mary Hallaren, others. Chronologies of engagements, more. Introduction. Addenda. 1,033 entries in alphabetical order. xi + 548pp. 6½ × 9¼. (Available in U.S. only)
24758-9 Pa. $11.95

LIFE IN ANCIENT EGYPT, Adolf Erman. Detailed older account, with much not in more recent books: domestic life, religion, magic, medicine, commerce, and whatever else needed for complete picture. Many illustrations. 597pp. 5⅜ × 8½.
22632-8 Pa. $8.50

HISTORIC COSTUME IN PICTURES, Braun & Schneider. Over 1,450 costumed figures shown, covering a wide variety of peoples: kings, emperors, nobles, priests, servants, soldiers, scholars, townsfolk, peasants, merchants, courtiers, cavaliers, and more. 256pp. 8⅜ × 11¼.
23150-X Pa. $7.95

THE NOTEBOOKS OF LEONARDO DA VINCI, edited by J. P. Richter. Extracts from manuscripts reveal great genius; on painting, sculpture, anatomy, sciences, geography, etc. Both Italian and English. 186 ms. pages reproduced, plus 500 additional drawings, including studies for *Last Supper, Sforza* monument, etc. 860pp. 7⅞ × 10⅝. (Available in U.S. only) 22572-0, 22573-9 Pa., Two-vol. set $25.90

AMERICAN CLIPPER SHIPS: 1833–1858, Octavius T. Howe & Frederick C. Matthews. Fully-illustrated, encyclopedic review of 352 clipper ships from the period of America's greatest maritime supremacy. Introduction. 109 halftones. 5 black-and-white line illustrations. Index. Total of 928pp. 5⅜ × 8½.
25115-2, 25116-0 Pa., Two-vol. set $17.90

TOWARDS A NEW ARCHITECTURE, Le Corbusier. Pioneering manifesto by great architect, near legendary founder of "International School." Technical and aesthetic theories, views on industry, economics, relation of form to function, "mass-production spirit," much more. Profusely illustrated. Unabridged translation of 13th French edition. Introduction by Frederick Etchells. 320pp. 6⅛ × 9¼. (Available in U.S. only) 25023-7 Pa. $8.95

THE BOOK OF KELLS, edited by Blanche Cirker. Inexpensive collection of 32 full-color, full-page plates from the greatest illuminated manuscript of the Middle Ages, painstakingly reproduced from rare facsimile edition. Publisher's Note. Captions. 32pp. 9⅜ × 12¼. 24345-1 Pa. $4.50

BEST SCIENCE FICTION STORIES OF H. G. WELLS, H. G. Wells. Full novel *The Invisible Man*, plus 17 short stories: "The Crystal Egg," "Aepyornis Island," "The Strange Orchid," etc. 303pp. 5⅜ × 8½. (Available in U.S. only)
21531-8 Pa. $4.95

AMERICAN SAILING SHIPS: Their Plans and History, Charles G. Davis. Photos, construction details of schooners, frigates, clippers, other sailcraft of 18th to early 20th centuries—plus entertaining discourse on design, rigging, nautical lore, much more. 137 black-and-white illustrations. 240pp. 6⅛ × 9¼.
24658-2 Pa. $5.95

ENTERTAINING MATHEMATICAL PUZZLES, Martin Gardner. Selection of author's favorite conundrums involving arithmetic, money, speed, etc., with lively commentary. Complete solutions. 112pp. 5⅜ × 8½. 25211-6 Pa. $2.95
THE WILL TO BELIEVE, HUMAN IMMORTALITY, William James. Two books bound together. Effect of irrational on logical, and arguments for human immortality. 402pp. 5⅜ × 8½. 20291-7 Pa. $7.50

THE HAUNTED MONASTERY and THE CHINESE MAZE MURDERS, Robert Van Gulik. 2 full novels by Van Gulik continue adventures of Judge Dee and his companions. An evil Taoist monastery, seemingly supernatural events; overgrown topiary maze that hides strange crimes. Set in 7th-century China. 27 illustrations. 328pp. 5⅜ × 8½. 23502-5 Pa. $5.00

CELEBRATED CASES OF JUDGE DEE (DEE GOONG AN), translated by Robert Van Gulik. Authentic 18th-century Chinese detective novel; Dee and associates solve three interlocked cases. Led to Van Gulik's own stories with same characters. Extensive introduction. 9 illustrations. 237pp. 5⅜ × 8½.
23337-5 Pa. $4.95

Prices subject to change without notice.
Available at your book dealer or write for free catalog to Dept. GI, Dover Publications, Inc., 31 East 2nd St., Mineola, N.Y. 11501. Dover publishes more than 175 books each year on science, elementary and advanced mathematics, biology, music, art, literary history, social sciences and other areas.